Hiking Waterfalls in Minnesota

HELP US KEEP THIS GUIDE UP TO DATE

Every effort has been made by the author and editors to make this guide as accurate and useful as possible. However, many things can change after a guide is published—trails are rerouted, regulations change, facilities come under new management, and so forth.

We would love to hear from you concerning your experiences with this guide and how you feel it could be improved and kept up to date. While we may not be able to respond to all comments and suggestions, we'll take them to heart, and we'll also make certain to share them with the author. Please send your comments and suggestions to the following address:

FalconGuides
Reader Response/Editorial Department
246 Goose Lane, Suite 200
Guilford, CT 06437

Or you may e-mail us at:

editorial@falcon.com

Thanks for your input, and happy trails!

Hiking Waterfalls in Minnesota

A Guide to the State's Best Waterfall Hikes

Steve Johnson

FALCONGUIDES

GUILFORD, CONNECTICUT

FALCONGUIDES®

An imprint of The Rowman & Littlefield Publishing Group, Inc.
4501 Forbes Blvd., Ste. 200
Lanham, MD 20706
www.rowman.com

Falcon and FalconGuides are registered trademarks and Make Adventure Your Story is a trademark of The Rowman & Littlefield Publishing Group, Inc.

Distributed by NATIONAL BOOK NETWORK

British Library Cataloguing in Publication Information available

Library of Congress Cataloging-in-Publication Data

Names: Johnson, Steve, 1965- author.
Title: Hiking waterfalls in Minnesota : a guide to the state's best waterfall hikes / Steve Johnson.
Description: Guilford, Connecticut : FalconGuides, 2018. | Includes index. | Identifiers: LCCN 2017049280 (print) | LCCN 2017050827 (ebook) | ISBN 9781493030200 (e-book) | ISBN 9781493030200 (pbk.) | ISBN 9781493030217 (ebook)
Subjects: LCSH: Hiking—Minnesota—Guidebooks. | Waterfalls—Minnesota—Guidebooks. | Trails—Minnesota—Guidebooks. | Minnesota—Guidebooks.
Classification: LCC GV199.42.M6 (ebook) | LCC GV199.42.M6 J65 2018 (print) | DDC 796.5109776—dc23
LC record available at https://lccn.loc.gov/2017049280

∞™ The paper used in this publication meets the minimum requirements of American National Standard for Information Sciences—Permanence of Paper for Printed Library Materials, ANSI/NISO Z39.48-1992.

Printed in the United States of America

The author and The Rowman & Littlefield Publishing Group, Inc., assume no liability for accidents happening to, or injuries sustained by, readers who engage in the activities described in this book.

Contents

The Hikes

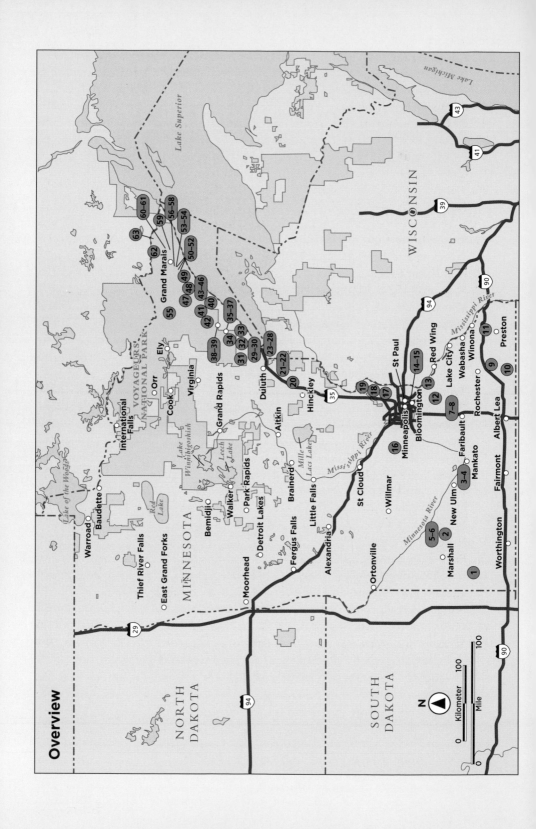

Overview

Acknowledgments

A book like this is a lot of fun to write. Really, traveling around the state ogling waterfalls is not too bad a deal. A book like this also requires the considerable talents of real pros. The aforementioned traveling and ogling is bookended by countless hours of research and editing. I've been fortunate to work with the incomparable staff at Globe Pequot for a bunch of years, and they nail it every time.

Big thanks go to my editor David Legere for guiding this book from a good idea to a full-on celebration of Minnesota's finest. One look at the maps on the following pages is all it takes to raise a glass to Melissa Baker. Her otherworldly skills turned my geographical scribbles into something you can actually use to find the falls. All the copy editors and graphics gang are hereby granted enthusiastic applause from now to the end of time. You're all amazing.

Every time I write a where-to book like this, it is filled with priceless intel or anecdotes from an unexpected supporting cast. Thanks to the always-eager staff at our state parks, and the jovial local from Hovland who told me a story about Portage Falls. Thanks to fellow hikers who know a thing or two about finding real gems along the trails. The girls at the Wolf Creek swimming hole helped me find the way back, and the bartender in Silver Bay knew a back way in to that place out yonder.

Brayden Mills and Jim Hoffman staked out more than one hundred waterfalls and captured them all to bring you frame-worthy photos throughout the book. Their work here will inspire you to go see our state's very best.

I had last-minute, save-the-day help from Cassandra Baltes and Stacy Dorn. Couldn't have done it without ya!

Thanks, mom and dad, for keeping me fueled with rhubarb pie and fresh blueberries.

Special thanks to all of you, for joining me in getting Out There.

Introduction

Minnesota rightly stakes claim to lots of water within its borders. Indeed, well over 10,000 lakes paint a good share of the state in shades of placid blue. But there are also close to 7,000 rivers, and rivers mean moving water, often appearing in various forms of falling. Our state is home to several hundred waterfalls, some small and quiet, others big and noisy. Lots of them allow very easy access—within sight of a car window for quick road trip distractions, standing on a highway bridge right on top of the falls, or at the end of an easygoing hike. Some waterfalls might require longer treks of a mile or three, and others are remote and mysterious, discovered only by canoeing and portaging your way through the great northern wilderness.

Minnesota's waterfalls all have something special to offer. They each have a style and grace all their own—distinct personalities that inspire, enthuse, and seduce. One waterfall might be restless or violent with spring rains. Another is busy, darting around boulders and fallen logs. Some are elegant veils, and still more are shy and reluctant to emerge from hiding. When visiting Minnesota's waterfalls, look at how so many of them seem to match their surroundings. A waterfall in a big city seems to appear regal and cosmopolitan, complementing the tall buildings and go-get-'em lifestyle; a falls in a forested, rocky gorge typically exudes a quieter beauty.

Join us on a tour of Minnesota, from the far southwest to the rolling bluffs of the Driftless Area, through metro-area cities and central regions, to Duluth and the unforgettable North Shore, and beyond to the Boundary Waters Canoe Area Wilderness. We'll explore waterfalls large and small; in remote, wild lands, tranquil parks, and busy urban centers, all the while uncovering lots of secrets and making acquaintance with some of the state's most dramatic nature in motion.

This book is arranged by region from south to north and highlights some of the showiest waterfalls in the state. Each entry is introduced by an information block outlining the name and location of the falls and waterway, hike distance and difficulty, applicable maps, GPS coordinates and directions for trailheads, contact information, and other beta. As far as gear and supplies, the best thing about "waterfalling" is there are no complicated gear concerns. Just throw on decent footwear, proper clothing, and away you go. Plan ahead, though, to make each visit a good one. Expect weather common to the area, and pack accordingly. Bring extra water to the drier, warmer southern regions, and be ready for cold winds and impromptu rainstorms (and snow!) along the North Shore. On longer hikes, your feet will be happier inside sturdy shoes or hiking boots, and take along snacks or a veritable grocery cart of grub for picnics at trailside overlooks or wooded campsites. Don't forget a camera or other photo device to take home the sights and sounds of the waterfalls. Keep in mind that water levels and seasons have a big impact on waterfalls' appearance and approachability. A lazy cascade in autumn could be a raging torrent in spring.

Stay safe around the falls. Sometimes it's just plain irresistible to take one more step for a closer look, but that urge might send you on a long fall to a really hard or really wet landing. A little slip into a stream might leave you with just a soggy foot, but take care so your favorite waterfall trips don't include anything worse than that.

Northland-bred scribe and tireless outdoor recreation junkie Steve Johnson shares his explorations and ruminations, complemented by vivid, inspiring images from Twin Cities photographers Brayden Mills and Jim Hoffman. We hope you enjoy our efforts to bring you up close to Minnesota's liquid landscapes. Let's go make some memories!

How to Use This Guide

This a fun book with zest matching its subject. You will find this guide contains just about everything you need to choose, plan for, and enjoy a waterfall hike in Minnesota. Packed with specific area information, *Hiking Waterfalls in Minnesota* features sixty-three mapped and cued hikes leading to over one hundred waterfalls, grouped together geographically. Here is an outline of the book's major components:

Each hike starts with a short **summary** of the hike's highlights. These quick overviews give you a taste of the hiking adventures and the waterfalls to be visited. You'll learn about the trail terrain and what highlights each route has to offer. Following the overview are **hike specs**—quick, nitty-gritty details of not only the waterfall but also the hike to it:

Waterway: The river or stream in which the waterfall resides.

Waterfall beauty: This is a 1 to 5 number, 5 being jaw-agape gorgeous.

Distance: The total distance of the recommended route; out and back, loops, and lollipop routes are included in this guide.

Difficulty: Each hike has been assigned a level of difficulty; easy, moderate, or difficult. The rating system was developed from several sources and personal experience. These levels are meant to be a guideline only and may prove easier or harder for different people depending on ability and physical fitness. For purposes of this book, an easy waterfall hike will generally cover 2 miles or less total trip distance, with minimal elevation gain, and a paved or smooth-surfaced dirt trail. A moderate waterfall hike will cover 3 to 5 miles total trip distance in one day, with moderate elevation gain and potentially rough terrain. A difficult hike may cover 5 or more miles total trip distance in one day, have difficult elevation gains, or have rough or rocky terrain.

Hiking time: The average time it will take to cover the route. It is based on the total distance, elevation gain, and condition and difficulty of the trail. Your fitness level will also affect your time.

Trail surface: General information about what to expect underfoot.

Other trail users: Such as horseback riders, mountain bikers, inline skaters, etc.

Canine compatibility: Know the trail regulations before you take your dog hiking with you. Dogs are typically allowed when leashed for the waterfall hikes in this book.

Land status: City park, state park, national park or forest, etc.

Fees and permits: Denotes park entrance fees and permits.

Maps: This is a list of other maps to supplement the maps in this book. USGS maps are the best source for accurate topographical information, but local park maps may show trails that are more recent. Use both.

Trail contacts: This is the location, phone number, and website URL for the local land manager(s) in charge of all the trails within the selected hike. Get trail access information before you head out, or contact the land manager after your visit if you see problems with trail erosion, damage, or misuse.

The **Finding the trailhead** section gives you dependable driving directions to trailheads. This also includes GPS trailhead coordinates for accurate navigation. **The Hike** is the meat of the chapter. Detailed and honest, it is a carefully researched impression of the waterfall, the hike, and interesting things you may see along the way, both natural and human. Under **Miles and Directions,** mileage cues identify all turns and trail name changes, as well as points of interest. **Sidebars** are found throughout the book and are quick and often fascinating facts about the locale. A detailed and expertly crafted **map** is included with each hike and is derived from GPS tracks and related field data while on the hikes.

Enjoy your outdoor exploration of Minnesota's waterfalls, and remember to pack out what you pack in.

How to Use the Maps

Overview map: This map shows the location of each hike in the area by hike number.

Route map: This is your primary guide to each hike. It shows the waterfalls, all the access roads and trails, points of interest, water, landmarks, and geographical features. It also distinguishes trails from roads, and paved roads from unpaved roads. The selected route is highlighted, and directional arrows point the way.

Trail Finder

To get our readers started on the hikes best suited to their interests and abilities, the following trail finder categorizes each of the hikes into a helpful list. Your favorite hikes might appear in more than one category.

Hike #/Name	Hikes to Tall Waterfalls	Hikes to Secluded Waterfalls	Easy-to-Reach Waterfalls	Kid-Friendly Waterfalls	Hikes for Nature Lovers	Hikes for Back-Packers
1. Winnewissa Falls—Pipestone National Monument	•			•		
2. Red Rock Falls		•	•		•	
3. Minneopa Falls—Minneopa State Park	•		•	•		
4. Minnemishinona Falls	•		•	•	•	
5. Ramsey Falls	•		•	•		
6. Redwood Falls			•	•		
7. Caron Falls		•	•	•	•	
8. Hidden Falls—Nerstrand Big Woods State Park		•	•		•	
9. Root River Falls	•		•	•		
10. Niagara Falls	•	•	•			
11. Pickwick Falls			•	•		
12. Little Cannon Falls			•	•		
13. Vermillion Falls	•		•	•		
14. Hidden Falls		•	•	•	•	

Hike #/Name	Hikes to Tall Waterfalls	Hikes to Secluded Waterfalls	Easy-to-Reach Waterfalls	Kid-Friendly Waterfalls	Hikes for Nature Lovers	Hikes for Back-Packers
15. Minnehaha Falls	•			•		
16. St. Anthony Falls			•	•		
17. Fairy Falls	•	•			•	
18. Marine Mill Falls			•	•		
19. Curtain Falls—Interstate State Park		•			•	
20. Big Spring Falls and Wolf Creek Falls—Banning State Park		•			•	
21. Swinging Bridge Falls and St. Louis Falls—Jay Cooke State Park			•		•	•
22. Oldenburg Cascades—Jay Cooke State Park		•			•	•
23. Kingsbury Creek Falls			•	•		
24. Falls of Miller Creek			•	•		
25. Falls of Chester Creek		•	•	•		
26. Falls of Tischer Creek		•	•	•	•	
27. Falls of Amity Creek—Amity and Lester Parks		•	•	•	•	
28. Falls of Lester River—Lester Park	•	•	•	•	•	

Hike #/Name	Hikes to Tall Waterfalls	Hikes to Secluded Waterfalls	Easy-to-Reach Waterfalls	Kid-Friendly Waterfalls	Hikes for Nature Lovers	Hikes for Back-Packers
29. French River Falls	•		•	•	•	
30. Trestle Bridge Falls			•	•	•	
31. Schmidt Creek Falls		•	•	•	•	
32. First Falls			•	•		
33. Second Falls		•		•	•	
34. Middle and Lower Falls—Gooseberry Falls State Park	•		•	•	•	
35. Upper and Fifth Falls—Gooseberry Falls State Park	•	•	•	•	•	•
36. Nelsens Creek Falls—Gooseberry Falls State Park		•				
37. Falls of Split Rock River		•	•	•	•	
38. Split Rock Creek Falls—Split Rock Lighthouse State Park		•		•	•	
39. Beaver River Falls			•	•		
40. Upper Beaver Falls		•	•		•	
41. Glen Avon Falls		•	•	•	•	
42. High Falls and Two Step Falls—Tettegouche State Park	•		•		•	•

Hike #/Name	Hikes to Tall Waterfalls	Hikes to Secluded Waterfalls	Easy-to-Reach Waterfalls	Kid-Friendly Waterfalls	Hikes for Nature Lovers	Hikes for Back-Packers
43. Cascade Falls—Tettegouche State Park		•		•	•	
44. Shovel Point Falls—Tettegouche State Park		•	•	•	•	
45. Illgen Falls—Tettegouche State Park	•		•	•	•	
46. Falls of Manitou River—George H. Crosby Manitou State Park		•			•	•
47. Falls of Caribou River	•	•			•	•
48. Two Island Falls			•	•	•	
49. Cross River Cascade			•	•	•	
50. Falls of Temperance River—Temperance River State Park	•	•	•	•	•	
51. Onion River Falls	•		•	•	•	
52. Upper Falls—Poplar River	•	•	•	•	•	•
53. Lower Falls—Poplar River			•	•	•	
54. Thompson Falls		•	•	•	•	•
55. Cascade Falls and The Cascades—Cascace River State Park	•		•	•	•	•
56. Hidden Falls—Cascade River			•	•	•	•

Hike #/Name	Hikes to Tall Waterfalls	Hikes to Secluded Waterfalls	Easy-to-Reach Waterfalls	Kid-Friendly Waterfalls	Hikes for Nature Lovers	Hikes for Back-Packers
57. Rosebush Falls	●		●	●	●	
58. Falls of Kadunce River		●	●	●	●	
59. Lower Falls—Judge C.R. Magney State Park		●			●	●
60. Upper Falls and Devils Kettle—Judge C.R. Magney State Park	●	●				●
61. Portage Falls		●	●	●	●	●
62. High Falls—Grand Portage State Park	●		●	●	●	
63. Middle Falls—Grand Portage State Park		●	●	●	●	●

Boundary Waters Canoe Area Wilderness and Border Country						
Kawishiwi Falls	●		●	●	●	
Dry Falls	●					
Vermillion Falls		●	●	●	●	
Seagull Falls		●	●	●	●	
Big Falls		●	●	●	●	
Little American Falls				●	●	

MAP LEGEND

Municipal

95   Freeway/Interstate Highway

25   US Highway

46   State Road

632   County/Other/Forest Road

– – – –   Gravel Road

▬▬▬▬   Featured Route

- - - - - -   Trail

Water Features

Pond/Lake

River or Creek

Waterfall

Land Management

State/County/Local Park

Symbols

Boat Ramp

Bridge

Cabin

Campground

Campsite (Backcountry)

Church

General Point of Interest

P   Parking

▲   Peak

Picnic Area

Ranger Station

Restroom

Scenic View/Viewpoint

Shelter

Swimming

1   Trailhead

?   Visitor/Information Center

Southern Minnesota

The southern areas of our state introduce wildly different personalities. Wide-open prairies and remnant grasslands from generations past punctuate much of the southwest and south-central, along with vast acres of fertile and very active agriculture lands stretching to each horizon. Sprawling farmsteads mark squares and rectangles of busy commercial efforts, with small, family farms firmly rooted hither and yon. Rolling hills of prairie grass, sporadic oak savannas, and ribbons of aged forests hearken back to Minnesota's younger years. Verdant river valleys curl along the paths of their respective waterways, providing essential life to crops, towns, and a rich variety of wildlife species. Rocky gorges appear unexpectedly on the lee of a hill or deep in a wood, formed of the eternal cut of a stream or river course following an ancient glacial retreat. Dakota Indian history is prevalent throughout the area, with historic sites and present-day influence commonplace, offering visitors a look at a proud heritage and influential time in the state's nascent history.

The lumpy landscape of the far southeast is magical, with bulbous, forested bluffs as far as you can see and intimate creeks and meadowlands tucked between. Idyllic hamlets as charming as your favorite fairy tale dot this scenic part of our state, with ski and bike trails, hiking destinations, and loads of popular campgrounds.

A generations-proud ethnic heritage defines small towns from border to border, with lively festivals of many varieties, like Mankato's Spring Fest, Albert Lea's Big Island Rendezvous, Montgomery's Kolacky Days, the German Mardi Gras in New Ulm, and Whalen's Stand-Still Parade. Don't miss the National Eagle Center in Wabasha, underground cave tours, vibrant arts scenes, and enough farmers' markets to fill your table with deliciousness all year round.

1 Winnewissa Falls–
Pipestone National Monument

Hike through historical and living Native American culture, where a centuries-old tradition of ceremonial pipe making still thrives. This paved, wheelchair-accessible path meanders past many of the monument's significant historical, cultural, and natural features.

Waterway: Pipestone Creek
Waterfall beauty: 3.5
Distance: 1-mile loop
Difficulty: Easy
Hiking time: About 1 hour
Trail surface: Paved and natural
Other trail users: None
Canine compatibility: Leashed pets allowed

Land status: National monument
Fees and permits: Fee required
Maps: Pipestone National Monument map;
USGS Pipestone North
Trail contacts: Pipestone National Monument,
36 Reservation Ave., Pipestone 56164,
(507) 825-5464 ext. 214, www.nps.gov/pipe

Finding the trailhead: From Pipestone, follow US 75 north to 111th Street (Reservation Avenue) and follow the road west for 1.2 miles to the Pipestone National Monument entrance.
Trailhead GPS: N44 00.796' / W96 19.525'

The Hike

Catlinite, or "pipestone," quite literally is the stone used for making ceremonial pipes. This red-hued stone, held sacred by Native Americans for hundreds of years, is still quarried today, and Pipestone National Monument is named for this stone and its tradition among native people.

The 1-mile Circle Trail leads past the quarry to Winnewissa Falls. The waterfall appears out of place in the rolling, treeless prairie of southwestern Minnesota. Natural fires once burned freely in this area, but early settlers' attempts to control the burns allowed trees and shrubs to grow near Pipestone Creek. Today the creek follows a serpentine forest of oak and cottonwood, winding through a vast sea of grasses. In a gust of moving water, the creek tumbles gently over a bluff of pink Sioux quartzite into a shaded glen of jumbled boulders. The appearance of the waterfall itself has changed, as well. To increase farming acreage upstream, the top 8 feet of rock at the brink of the falls were blasted away in the early 1900s. Despite these man-made alterations, Winnewissa, a Sioux term for "jealous maiden," remains an inviting destination.

To reach the waterfall, follow the Circle Trail from the west doors of the visitor center. The short, paved trail is an easy walk and starts with a stroll through native

Winnewissa Falls tumbles through a shallow gorge. JIM HOFFMAN

tallgrass prairie. The clockwise loop soon crosses Pipestone Creek, meanders past one of the small, actively mined pipestone quarries, and reenters the wooded creek bed downstream of the falls. At a trail fork below the falls, take the path up a short set of stone stairs to the crest of the low bluff. From here, not far from where explorer Joseph N. Nicollet carved his signature into the rock in 1838, enjoy an unobstructed view of the waterfall, framed by green oak leaves and yellow-pink bedrock. The water falls about 20 feet in a wide curtain into a craggy alcove of gray rock, with several massive boulders in the creek below. The trail continues to the top of the falls and descends a stone stairway to the asphalt bridge traversing Pipestone Creek at the waterfall's base. From here you gain a great look at the beauty of the creek and its falls, and a final trek on the trail crosses an expanse of meadow maintained as native prairie by frequent controlled burns.

Pipestone National Monument preserves not only the human history of the site, but a variety of natural features, as well. Both the forest floor and open prairie bloom with wildflowers in spring through fall, including Canada violet, yellow ladyslipper, wild columbine, fringed sagebrush, and purple prairie clover. Birds of many species thrive here, too, including the western meadowlark and ring-necked pheasant,

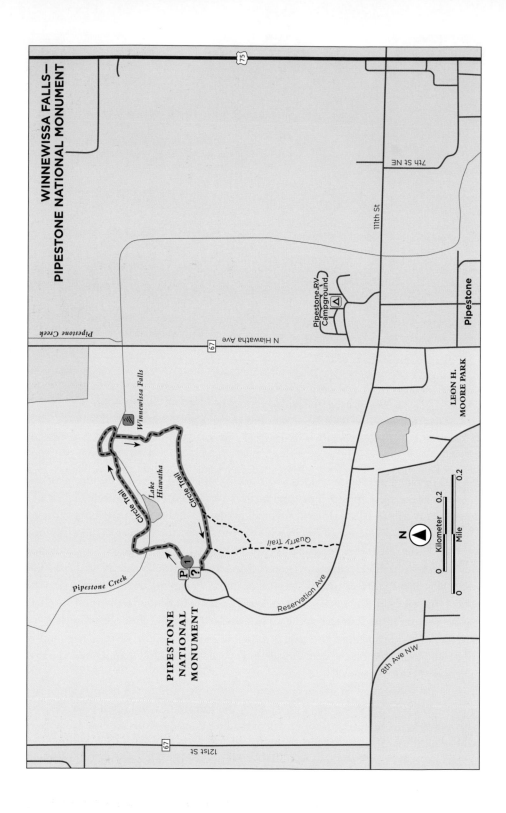

WINNEWISSA FALLS—
PIPESTONE NATIONAL MONUMENT

Square-faced rock walls flank Winnewissa Falls. BRAYDEN MILLS

water-loving birds like the red-winged blackbird and belted kingfisher, and wood-land birds such as the black-capped chickadee and common flicker.

The visitor center maintains exhibits describing pipestone quarrying and carving, as well as the natural and cultural history of the region. A Native American stone carver's facility resides under the same roof, providing demonstrations of native crafts construction.

Miles and Directions

0.0 Hike north from the trailhead at the visitor center.

0.3 Cross Pipestone Creek.

0.5 Go left at the sign for Old Stone Face.

0.6 Follow the path down the stairs for a creek-level view of the falls.

0.7 Spur trail to the Oracle, a rock formation resembling a face, of spiritual significance to native tribes.

0.98 Junction with the Quarry Trail; continue straight on the Circle Trail.

1.0 Arrive back at the trailhead.

For about 3,000 years, Native American plains tribes held sacred the site of today's Pipestone National Monument as the go-to source for pipestone. Tribes of all walks traveled here to quarry the stone, and even enemy tribes worked together to harvest the prized red rock.

2 Red Rock Falls

In the midst of wide-open rolling prairie, discover this grotto of raggedy stone cliffs shaped by Mound Creek's inexorable sculpting. The slender waterfall skips off ledges to a quiet pool, with informal trails tailor made for free-spirited exploring.

Waterway: Mound Creek
Waterfall beauty: 4
Distance: 0.2 mile out and back
Difficulty: Easy
Hiking time: 15 minutes
Trail surface: Mowed grass
Other trail users: None
Canine compatibility: Leashed pets allowed

Land status: County park
Fees and permits: No fee required
Maps: County park map; USGS Sanborn SE
Trail contacts: Cottonwood County Parks, 1355 9th Ave., Windom 56101, (507) 831-1389, www.co.cottonwood.mn.us/county-departments/parks

Finding the trailhead: From Windom, follow US 71 north for 19 miles to 250th Street. Turn right and head east for 0.8 mile to the parking area on the right.
Trailhead GPS: N44 07.346' / W95 06.273'
Note: The park is open from May 1 to October 31.

The Hike

Red Rock Falls is a delight for travelers, geology fans, and adventurous kids and hikers. In what seems like the middle of endless farm fields, Mound Creek finds its way into a fairy-tale grotto of forest and rugged sandstone cliffs in all manner of otherworldly forms. It is a stunning setting and a wonderful destination to explore, with crannies and nooks at every turn. There is no formal trail system here, but a network of established social trails leads to the area's most alluring attractions.

The creek snakes into the gorge and over jumbles of boulders to a "where did this come from?" 30-foot waterfall gliding to a secluded pool below. Cliffs stained with moss and lichen flank the pool. The slender and very pretty waterfall reveals an elegance as it slips down the crease in the rocks. The creek takes a hard right at the bottom of the falls, and the shallow pool is great for a refreshing swim on sweltering summer days.

Close to Red Rock Falls is the Jeffers Petroglyphs site, just 4 miles southeast. This Minnesota Historical Site is home to fascinating Native American petroglyphs preserved in islands of exposed rock.

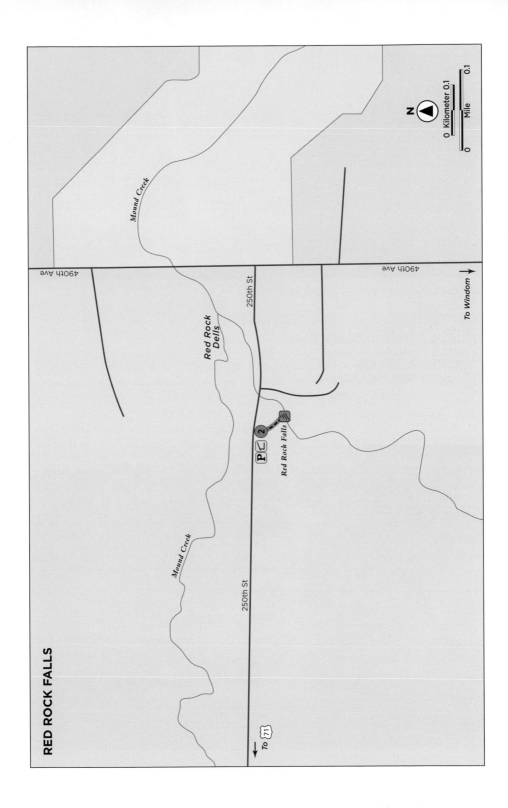

RED ROCK FALLS

Red Rock Falls and its craggy grotto. JIM HOFFMAN

Miles and Directions

0.0 Parking area trailhead. Hike past the west side of the shelter and listen for the falls. Continue straight ahead to follow perimeter trails on the other side of the gorge. Just roam the social trails for as long or short as you like.

0.2 Arrive at trailhead.

Red Rock Falls. BRAYDEN MILLS

3 Minneopa Falls–Minneopa State Park

Among a landscape of oak savanna, hardwood forest, grassland, and river floodplain, Minneopa State Park offers a variety of attractions to complement the scenic falls, including a vigorous wildlife population, hiking trails, and resident bison herd.

Waterway: Minneopa Creek
Waterfall beauty: 5
Distance: About 1.2 miles out and back
Difficulty: Easy
Hiking time: About 30 minutes
Trail surface: Mix of paved, natural, and stone
Other trail users: None
Canine compatibility: Leashed pets allowed

Land status: State park
Fees and permits: Fee required
Maps: Minneopa State Park map; USGS Mankato West
Trail contacts: Minneopa State Park, 54497 Gadwall Rd., Mankato 56001, (507) 389-5464, www.dnr.state.mn.us/state_parks/minneopa

Finding the trailhead: From Mankato, follow US 169 west for 5 miles to MN 68 and follow signs to the park entrance. The trail to the falls starts at the parking area adjacent to the park office.
Trailhead GPS: N44 08.920' / W94 05.524'

The Hike

The Dakota Indians made their home in the area of the present-day park, and Minneopa in their language means "water falling twice." Indeed, Minneopa Creek curves lazily past sturdy historic stone buildings in the main picnic area, drops over a short ledge to swirl and eddy a bit around scattered rocks, and then plunges about 40 feet into a deep limestone gorge. The waterfall tumbles elegantly in a wide veil, with a stronger surge at one side fading to transparent vines at the curve of the gorge. Dense foliage of maple and oak forest line the ridge along the top, while vibrant green mosses and ferns drape the cliff slopes. An easy hike across the bridge from the picnic area leads to a nice view of the upper falls, and the path continues along the top of the gorge for a great look at the main falls and plunge pool below. A long stairway descends to creek level and another bridge leading to more hiking trails. The dirt footpath to the right, just before the bridge, leads over smooth rocks and roots along the creek's bank beneath a high canopy of sun-speckled leaves for a head-on view of the waterfall. Several large boulders perched in the creek are great lounge chairs for staying awhile in the heart of the scene.

While the falls are the park's highlight, the Seppmann windmill is another popular destination. Built just northwest of the falls in 1864, this was one of the first stone gristmills in Minnesota. Wind-powered grain milling was uncommon at the time, but the Seppmann Mill could grind 150 bushels of wheat into flour every day,

Minneopa Falls shows its stuff on a summer day. JIM HOFFMAN

and neighbors from 30 miles distant lugged their grist here for the mill's services. A tornado carried away two of the windmill's arms in 1880, hastening its decline in production. The windmill site is just a short hike from the park campground.

Minneopa State Park's distinct ecosystems support wonderfully diverse wildlife habitats, many of which can be spotted along the park's trails. Be on the lookout for the likes of eastern bluebirds, yellow-shafted flickers, meadowlarks, and pileated woodpeckers. Wild turkeys and ring-necked pheasants sneak through tall grasses, and the floodplain of the Minnesota River is home to beavers, belted kingfishers, fox squirrels, and waterfowl.

This area has a long tradition of human visitors enjoying the natural splendor as well. The tiny town of Minneopa Village was built here around 1870, and the falls attracted many people from surrounding communities for picnics and general frolicking. Some soirees caught the attention of pretty much everybody, and upwards of 5,000 people descended on the village for serious celebrating. Alas, the grasshopper plagues, hordes of a different ilk, wiped out the crops, and the little town disappeared after only a short time.

Miles and Directions

0.0 Follow the path from the trailhead to the big ol' bridge crossing the creek.

0.4 Cross the bridge, with views of the upper falls upstream.

MINNEOPA FALLS—MINNEOPA STATE PARK

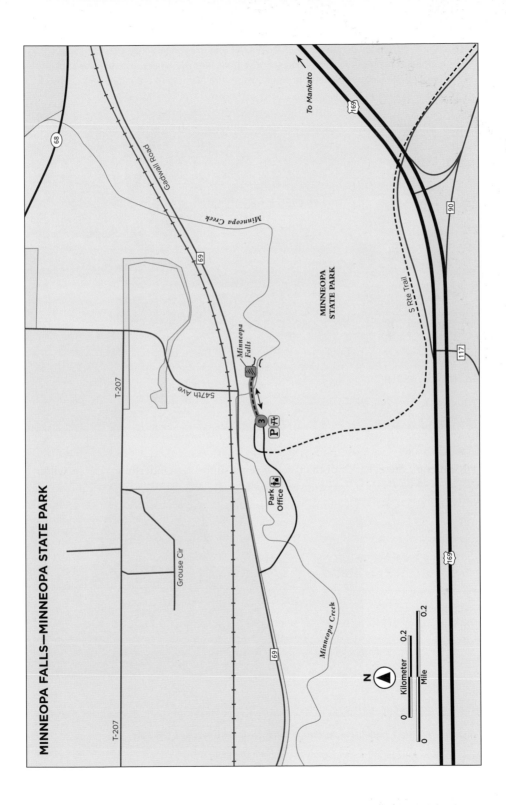

0.6 Follow the stone stairway down to creek level and a wooden bridge over the creek, for beauteous views of Minneopa Falls. Social trails lead closer the falls, but use caution on slippery surfaces. Return the same way up the stairway to the bridge and trailhead.

1.2 Arrive back at the trailhead.

Above: Afternoon sunshine bathes the upper falls. BRAYDEN MILLS
Right: The Seppmann windmill site at the park. JIM HOFFMAN

Established in 1905, Minneopa is Minnesota's third-oldest state park and includes a reintroduced bison herd roaming a sprawling enclosure northwest of the falls.

4 Minnemishinona Falls

Hidden away in a wooded ravine for generations until its transformation into a county park, Minnemishinona Falls now welcomes visitors from far and wide to its captivating scene.

Waterway: Minnesota River tributary
Waterfall beauty: 4
Distance: 0.8 mile out and back
Difficulty: Easy
Hiking time: About 10 minutes
Trail surface: Paved
Other trail users: Cyclists

Canine compatibility: Leashed pets allowed
Land status: County park
Fees and permits: No fee required
Maps: County park map; USGS Mankato West
Trail contacts: Nicollet County, 501 S. Minnesota Ave., St. Peter 56082, (507) 931-1760, www.co.nicollet.mn.us/349/Parks-Trails

Finding the trailhead: From Mankato, follow US 169 north to US 14, then head west on US 14 to CR 41. Go south on CR 41 (Rockford Road) for 1.5 miles to Judson Bottom Road. As the road curves right, the parking and falls area is on the left.
Trailhead GPS: N44 10.209' / W 94 05.099'

The Hike

A long-held local secret, largely unknown to most of us for decades, Nicollet County acquired this scenic falls area and opened it to the public in 2007. The three-acre county park now includes a picnic site and a bridge across the river and falls for excellent viewing. The paved trail across the falls heads toward Mankato as part of an extensive network of bike trail routes.

The Minnesota River Valley boasts a stunning landscape of wooded ravines and high bluffs overlooking expansive valleys cradling the river. Often overlooked by travelers and even seasoned natives, the river's long, winding course in this south-central region of the state holds mystery and adventure, and a who's who of very active and visible wildlife.

Tucked into one of the countless clefts in the river bluffs near Mankato, a small tributary ambles in from the west and, in an almost surprise moment, plunges 42 feet over a ledge. Embraced by a limestone cirque, the skinny waterfall drops into a small pool, eddies a bit, and then the creek continues on its way to meet the Minnesota River.

Common to many areas of the southern regions of Minnesota, plains and woodlands Indian tribes made their homes in this area. More than a half dozen burial mounds are located just north of Minnemishinona Falls.

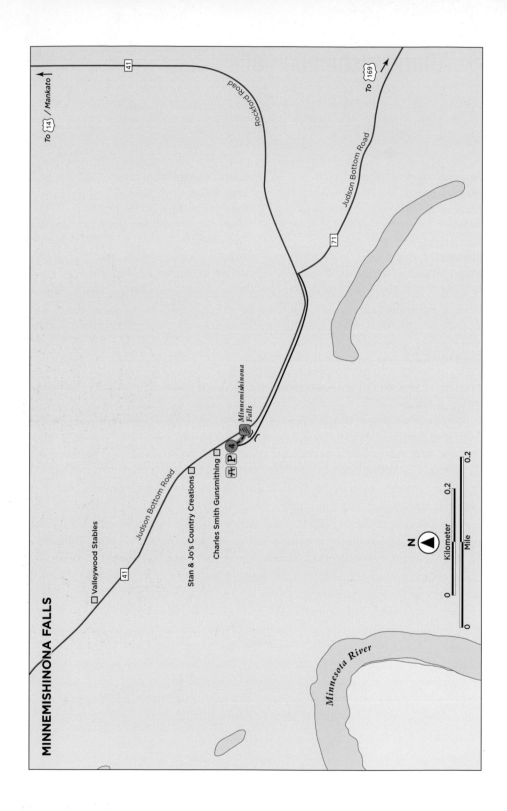

MINNEMISHINONA FALLS

Diminutive and secluded Minnemishinona Falls. BRAYDEN MILLS

Miles and Directions

0.0 From the trailhead, simply follow the path southeast to the bridge overlooking the creek and waterfall.

0.4 Reach the bridge.

0.8 Return to the trailhead.

5 Ramsey Falls

Set aside a full day to enjoy the sights and sounds of Alexander Ramsey Park. With two postcard-perfect waterfalls, 4 miles of hiking trails, and even a zoo, the hard part is deciding what to see next.

Waterway: Ramsey Creek
Waterfall beauty: 5
Distance: 0.1 mile (overlook is just steps from parking area)
Difficulty: Easy
Hiking time: About 5 minutes
Trail surface: Paved
Other trail users: None
Canine compatibility: Leashed pets allowed

Land status: City park
Fees and permits: No fee required
Maps: Redwood Falls park map; USGS Delhi
Trail contacts: City of Redwood Falls Parks and Recreation, 901 Cook St., Redwood Falls 56283, (507) 644-2333, www.redwoodareacommunitycenter.com/area-parks/alexander-ramsey-park

Finding the trailhead: From Bridge Street in Redwood Falls, follow North Grove Street for 0.2 mile to the park entrance. Take the park road to the junction with the spur road to the falls parking area.
Trailhead GPS: N44 32.744' / W95 07.534'

The Hike

A pair of unassuming judicial drainage ditches wander through open farmland in this area of southwestern Minnesota, keeping their distance for nearly 10 miles until the attraction becomes too great and they rendezvous just west of Redwood Falls, beginning new life as Ramsey Creek. The creek follows a lazy line to the outskirts of town, where it scrunches into tight oxbows and squiggles into Alexander Ramsey Park, known as the "Little Yellowstone of Minnesota." Here the creek rumbles and roars, plunging in a 45-foot waterfall into a rugged, wooded ravine, staking claim as the park's distinctive centerpiece. Named for the first governor of the Minnesota Territory, this is the largest city park in Minnesota, boasting native, wooded areas never cut or used for pasture. The area has been utilized as a picnic area and park continuously since 1886, including nearly 50 years as a Minnesota State Park.

There are 4 miles of hiking trails in the park, but we only need a small portion of that to reach the falls. A paved section of trail leads from the picnic area to a suspension bridge over a small ravine and then on to the falls overlook. Ramsey Creek is a clear, cool stream stocked with brown and rainbow trout, and Ramsey Falls itself flows between two 90-degree bends in the creek. Rock walls and foliage obstruct much of the river both upstream and down, creating the illusion that the water appears just

Ramsey Falls. JIM HOFFMAN ▶

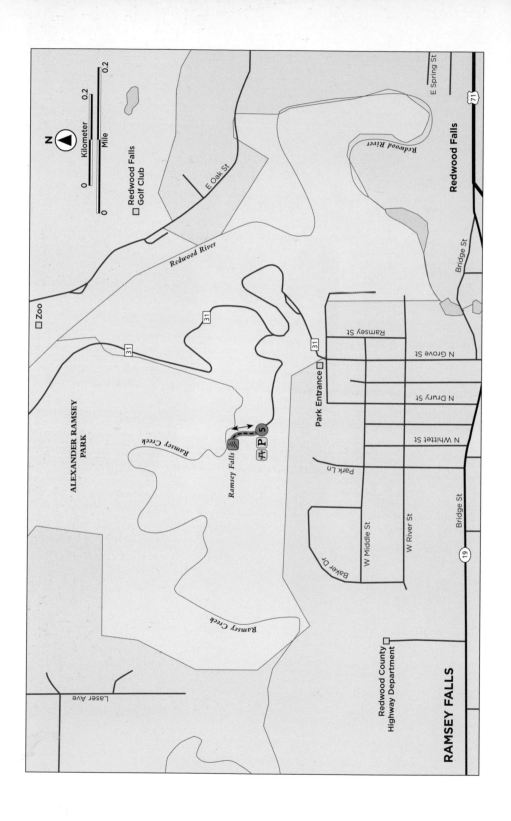

Center stage view of Ramsey Falls. BRAYDEN MILLS

in time to sail over the ledge, disappearing with equal haste around the bend. The overlook provides the best vantage for ogling the falls head-on, although access to the crest is possible via an unmaintained trail about 50 yards upstream of the overlook. The base of the falls is rendered inaccessible due to the precipitous cliffs dropping straight into the water, way down there.

While Ramsey Falls is the main attraction of the park, a variety of hiking trails access numerous other interests while meandering up and down the bluffs above Ramsey Creek and the Redwood River. The river tumbles over Redwood Falls (see Hike 6, Redwood Falls) along one boundary of the park, and below this falls is a wooded campground and small zoo, replete with animals formerly found throughout southern Minnesota, including elk, deer, bison, prairie dogs, and a variety of waterfowl.

Miles and Directions

0.0 Hike north from the trailhead.

0.1 Overlook of the falls, only steps from the parking area.

Tip: Start from one of the parking areas at the north side of the park for a longer hike to the waterfall.

Suspension footbridge at Ramsey Falls.
BRAYDEN MILLS

6 Redwood Falls

Two handsome waterfalls are within walking distance of each other. The city of Redwood Falls owns those enviable bragging rights, and both falls are right here in Alexander Ramsey Park.

Waterway: Redwood River
Waterfall beauty: 3.5
Distance: 0.2 mile out and back
Difficulty: Easy to moderate
Hiking time: About 10 minutes
Trail surface: Paved
Other trail users: None
Canine compatibility: Leashed pets allowed
Land status: City park

Fees and permits: No fee required
Maps: Redwood Falls park map; USGS Redwood Falls
Trail contacts: City of Redwood Falls Parks and Recreation, 901 Cook St., Redwood Falls 56283, (507) 644-2333, www.redwoodareacommunitycenter.com/ area-parks/alexander-ramsey-park

Finding the trailhead: From Bridge Street in Redwood Falls, follow North Grove Street for 0.2 mile to the park entrance. Take the park road to the Zeb Gray playground and shelter area.
Trailhead GPS: N44 32.744' / W95 07.275'

The Hike

A shorter sibling to Ramsey Falls, and the town's namesake, Redwood Falls cascades into a deep gorge just inside the park's entrance, only steps from the parking area and trailhead.

The Redwood River flows north and east from prairies and farmland into the valley carved originally by the great Glacial River Warren, now occupied by the Minnesota River. Redwood Falls is the central feature of the Redwood Cascades, a spirited stretch of river rapids in this large city park. All told, the Redwood River drops 140 feet to the valley floor, much of its descent in regulated fashion at the hands of several dams (the largest of which was built in 1902 and currently plugs the river at Lake Redwood), which have produced hydroelectric power from the falling waters since 1897. The falls itself originally powered a roller mill prior to being modified for hydro energy. Man-made intrusions aside, the picturesque bluffs flanking the river are a beauteous sight and form a fantastic natural retreat so close to town.

The waterfall is most easily viewed from the pedestrian bridge traversing the Redwood River just above the crest of the falls. From the Zeb Gray parking area, follow the trail into the woods past the picnic shelter perched on the bluff above the river. Continue downhill to the narrow iron and concrete bridge spanning from bluff to bluff above the falls. Looking upstream, the river gains strength, tumbling from the Lake Redwood Dam downward into the deepening valley. The town of Redwood

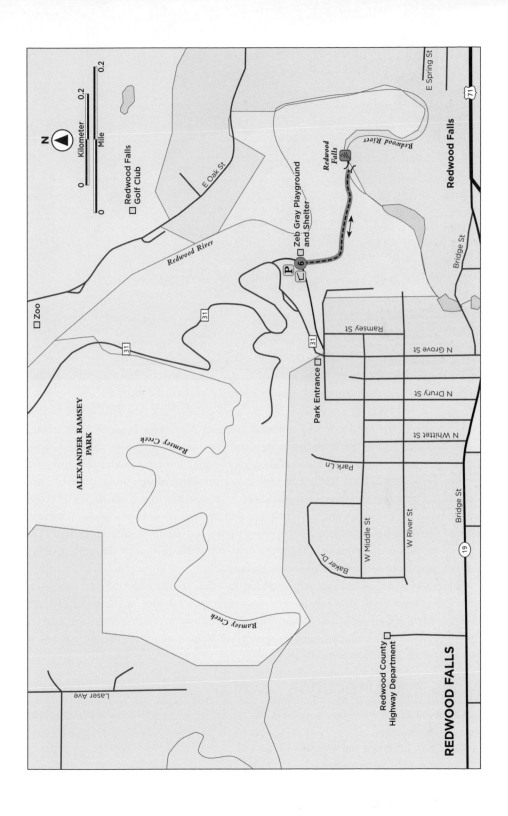

N

0   0.2   0.2
Kilometer

0   0.2
Mile

☐ Redwood Falls
   Golf Club

☐ Zoo

Redwood River

E Oak St

ALEXANDER RAMSEY
PARK

Ramsey Creek

Ramsey Creek

Laser Ave

31

31

31

Park Entrance ☐

Park Ln

Baker Dr

W Middle St

W River St

Ramsey St

N Grove St

N Drury St

N Whittet St

Bridge St

19

Redwood County
Highway Department ☐

REDWOOD FALLS

☐ Zeb Gray Playground
   and Shelter

P

6

Redwood
Falls

Redwood River

Redwood Falls

E Spring St

71

Bridge St

Redwood Falls steps lively through Alexander Ramsey Park. BRAYDEN MILLS

Falls overlooks the left bank and wooded bluffs of Alexander Ramsey Park on the right. Just after passing beneath the bridge, the river drops 3 feet over a smooth, concrete apron and then crashes ferociously into a single, massive boulder that splits the torrent in two for its final 12-foot tumble into a broad, swirling plunge pool. On one side of the boulder, the river catapults directly downward in a frothing jet of white water, while on the other the current takes a sharp turn to slide gracefully across the face of the rock before twisting back downstream for the final drop to its base. The base of the falls is easily reached from the east end of the bridge by scrambling down a short, unmaintained trail to the water's edge.

Clambering on weathered gray boulders to a finger-like point of land extending into the plunge pool, you can look almost directly upstream at the twin cataracts gliding around the intruding stone. The river follows a restless, swirling current downstream to sheer bluffs lining its west bank before winding placidly toward its junction with the Minnesota River.

Miles and Directions

0.0 Trailhead at the Zeb Gray playground and shelter. Follow the path down to a bridge spanning the falls.

0.1 Reach the bridge and waterfall.

0.2 Arrive back at the trailhead.

7 Caron Falls

Get heartbeat-quiet solitude at Caron Falls, a little-known gem secreted away at the back side of this small and crowd-free county park near Northfield.

Waterway: Prairie Creek
Waterfall beauty: 4
Distance: 0.8 mile out and back
Difficulty: Easy
Hiking time: About 30 minutes
Trail surface: Natural
Other trail users: None

Canine compatibility: Leashed pets allowed
Land status: County park
Fees and permits: No fee required
Maps: County park map; USGS Nerstrand
Trail contacts: Rice County Parks, 320 Third St. NW, Faribault 55021, (507) 332-6100, www.co.rice.mn.us/parks-facilities/caron-park

Finding the trailhead: From Northfield, follow MN 3 south for 2 miles to CR 20 (Cannon City Boulevard). Turn left and follow CR 20 for 3 miles to 145th Street (gravel). Turn left on 145th Street to Falk Avenue (first road from CR 20). Turn right on Falk Avenue and head south for 2.2 miles to 170th Street (CR 88). Turn left and go east for 0.8 mile to the park entrance.
Trailhead GPS: N44 20.799' / W93 09.885'

The Hike

Prior to settlement days in the 1930s, the sprawling expanse of maple-basswood forest known as the "Big Woods" covered over 5,000 square miles in a wide swath from Mankato to St. Cloud, including two-thirds of what later became Rice County. Agriculture claimed most of the woods, but remnant stands in southern Minnesota remain. One sixty-acre vestige lives on today thanks to the foresight of the Caron family, who once farmed this land. The Carons offered to sell forty acres to the county, adding to an existing twenty, and the park is named for family patriarch Ferdinand Caron.

Established in 1990, with development continuing through 1997, the diminutive Caron Park offers a very quiet getaway for visitors to this scenic region of the state. Concealed along a dusty gravel road past Northfield, Caron seems to appear suddenly and often elicits a double take from passersby when first seeing it. With only a small shelter and primitive restroom, on the surface there doesn't appear much to do here, but one only needs look to the trees to discover more.

West of the shelter, a trail leads into the woods, gradually descending through the shade of giant ash, maple, cottonwood, and other hardwood species. The sound of the waterfall reaches you first and when it does, follow the spur trail to the left. After a dozen steps or so, the trail reaches the creek and the elegant little waterfall. The creek drops off several small ledges at the crest, and then stretches out to tumble and cascade and drizzle over nooks and crannies of raggedy limestone in about a 5-foot

Peaceful and pretty Caron Falls. BRAYDEN MILLS

drop to a shallow pool. There is easy access to the top of the waterfall for up-close views, and the wading-friendly pool below is usually busy with frogs.

This is an especially relaxing waterfall, and with a number of made-to-order boulders and logs nearby, it's the perfect spot to sit a spell and let the peace of the place cure all that ails you. ***Caution:*** Mosquitoes rule these woods in summer. Bring bug spray lest your soothing interlude be cut short from blood loss. Target the early morning or wait for late fall when mosquitoes are not in such a frenzy.

About 100 yards upstream is a steel-frame bridge across the creek, which leads to the trail back to the shelter and to adjacent mountain bike trails. If you are a fan of fat tire riding, the local off-road cycling group—Cannon River Off-Road Cycling and Trails—built a frolicking good trail system here, with about 3 miles of flowy path winding through the woods.

Back at the trailhead, take a moment to admire and stroll through the restored meadow near the parking area. The area is lively with yellow prairie coneflower and pink trefoil and about fifty other wildflower personalities. Count on sharing your space with butterflies and hummingbirds and melodious songbirds, as well.

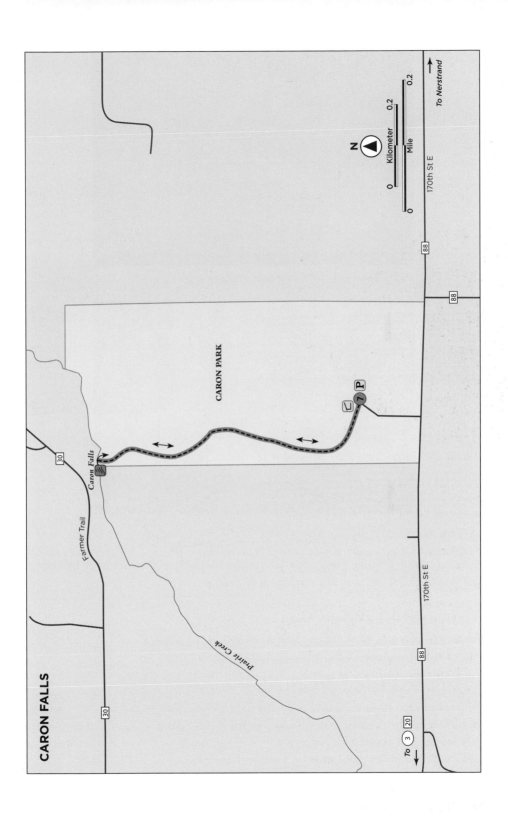

CARON FALLS

CARON PARK

Caron Falls

Farmer Trail

Prairie Creek

To ③ 20

170th St E

30

30

88

88

88

170th St E

To Nerstrand

P

N

Kilometer
0   0.2

Mile
0   0.2

Fallen leaves eddy below the falls. BRAYDEN MILLS

Trail bridge above Caron Falls. BRAYDEN MILLS

See Caron Falls at its most active in spring, when it swells with winter snowmelt, and during fall, when it glows red and gold with the trees.

Miles and Directions

0.0 Hike west from the trailhead to the trail leading into the woods.

0.4 Reach the waterfall. Cross the bridge to return.

0.8 Arrive back to the trailhead.

8 Hidden Falls–Nerstrand Big Woods State Park

Showy wildflowers, some rarely seen elsewhere, color the forest floor of this sprawling state park. Hidden Falls is tucked in the midst of it all, and is a popular go-to site on the park's hiking trails.

Waterway: Prairie Creek
Waterfall beauty: 3
Distance: 0.8 mile out and back
Difficulty: Easy
Hiking time: About 45 minutes
Trail surface: Natural
Other trail users: None
Canine compatibility: Leashed pets allowed

Land status: State park
Fees and permits: Fee required
Maps: Nerstrand Big Woods State Park map; USGS Nerstrand
Trail contacts: Nerstrand Big Woods State Park, 970 170th St. E., Nerstrand 55053, (507) 333-4840, www.dnr.state.mn.us/state_parks/nerstrand_big_woods/index.html

Finding the trailhead: From Northfield, follow MN 246 south to CR 29. Turn right and head west for 1.2 miles to the park entrance.
Trailhead GPS: N44 20.598' / W93 06.269'

The Hike

Hidden Falls is nestled in a deep, wooded valley in one of the last remaining stands of "Big Woods" vegetation in Minnesota. Dense, old-growth hardwood forest of ash, sugar maple, elm, and basswood blanket the area's rolling hills. Originally close to 5,000 acres in size, these woods were under imminent threat of logging saws during the 1930s, but even as soon as the early 1940s, preservation-minded people worked toward establishing the land as a state park. Within the park is a wonderful abundance of wildlife and over fifty varieties of wildflowers like bloodroot, Dutchman's breeches, and the dwarf trout lily. Eleven miles of trails roam among the trees and up and down ridges and through valleys of deep green ferns and vibrant understory foliage. As you wander the secluded hiking trails crisscrossing this preserved woodland, stay alert for local wildlife including deer, beavers, raccoons, and the ubiquitous grey, fox, and red squirrels. The park is also home to a wide range of migratory birds, in addition to a resident population of wild turkeys.

Prairie Creek flows through the northern half of the park, across a bed of Platteville limestone that was once the floor of an ancient shallow sea. Glacial meltwater spent eons cutting through a 150-foot-thick layer of glacial drift through this watershed to the horizontal stratum of limestone. As the creek meets a stack of flat, mossy rock ledges, a thin curtain of water drapes gently over the edge to a shallow pool

The bridal veil look of Hidden Falls. BRAYDEN MILLS

about 10 feet below. It is a soothing waterfall, and a handy log bench near the stream's edge is perfect for just sitting and listening to the water sing. The shallow plunge pool below the falls is great for wading on a hot summer day. If it's springtime, however, the falls often thunder over the crest in a muddy maelstrom of runoff from farmland upstream, especially for the first several days after a heavy rainstorm. Winter visitors often arrive at the falls on cross-country skis or snowshoes to see a spectacular wall of fused icicles. The stream's rumble echoing behind a frozen ice sheet is a special Minnesota cold-weather treat.

Big Woods Dairy was another highlight of the park from 1987 to 2006. The dairy was an eighty-acre sustainable farm owned by the state and leased to a family living on-site and operating a rotational-grazing dairy farm, the only modern working dairy farm in a state park in the United States. There were no row crops or pesticides here, and the only fertilizer was the natural kind provided by cows grazing in pastures divided by movable electric fences. By rotating the herd through divided pastures, the farm eliminated overgrazing, soil compaction, and debilitating erosion. When the lease on the land ended, the park removed the farm buildings and planted native trees and grasses in the pastures. Initiated as a sustainable agriculture demonstration project, Big Woods Dairy proved to be a resounding success and a testament to the coexistence of farming and natural resources.

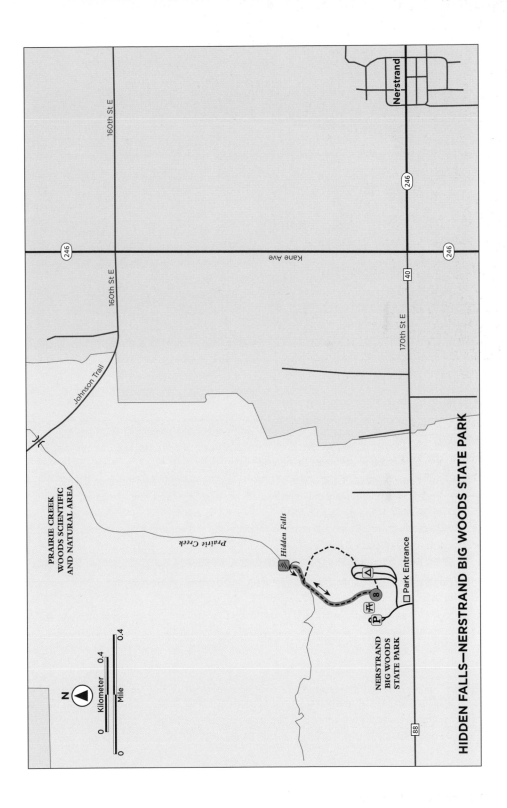

HIDDEN FALLS—NERSTRAND BIG WOODS STATE PARK

Hidden Falls cascades over a ragged limestone ledge. BRAYDEN MILLS

Miles and Directions

0.0 From the playground area near the park office, follow the hiking trail north into the woods. The path gradually descends through a forest of ash, basswood, hickory, aspen, and ubiquitous sugar maple to the valley and creek.

0.4 Arrive at the waterfall and bridge over the creek. Return to the trailhead on the same trail, or take an alternate and steeper path heading southeast from the creek.

0.8 Arrive back at the trailhead.

> The dwarf trout lily is a federally listed endangered wildflower and grows here in Minnesota (predominantly in the Cannon River watershed) and nowhere else on earth.

9 Root River Falls

Embraced in picturesque bluffs and serenaded by the Root River, Lanesboro is one of the most popular go-to towns in Minnesota for the full shop, dine, and get-active palette, with calendar-shot scenery in every direction.

Waterway: Root River
Waterfall beauty: 4-5
Distance: 0.2 mile out and back
Difficulty: Easy
Hiking time: About 10 minutes
Trail surface: Natural
Other trail users: None
Canine compatibility: Leashed pets allowed

Land status: City of Lanesboro
Fees and permits: No fee required
Maps: General Lanesboro city maps; USGS Lanesboro
Trail contacts: Lanesboro Visitor Center, 100 Milwaukee Rd., Lanesboro 55949, (507) 467-2696, lanesboro.com

Finding the trailhead: From Rochester, follow US 52 south to Fountain. Turn left (east) on CR 8 and head 8.5 miles to Lanesboro. Turn right on Parkway Avenue and head south to a right turn on Kirkwood Street. The waterfall is at the dam at the north end of the athletic fields and Riverview Campground. **Note:** Additional parking is available one-half block north of Kirkwood Street. **Trailhead GPS:** N43 42.991' / W91 58.681'

The Hike

Tucked in a pastoral pocket of the Root River Valley in Minnesota's southeastern corner, Lanesboro is one of the state's most beautiful towns. How can we go wrong with honors like the "Great American Main Street Award," one of the "100 Best Small Art Towns," and a top 50 placing in "Best Outdoor Sports Towns"? How about one of the "20 Best Dream Towns in America"? All this is evident with the first step into this fantastic town of quiet neighborhoods and scenic splendor. Wonderfully preserved gingerbread Victorian homes line the streets. Many of these now serve as dreamy bed-and-breakfasts. Majestic, 300-foot bluffs rise above town. Impeccably maintained buildings on Parkway Avenue house quaint shops, eateries, and art galleries. The magnificent Root River Trail winds right through town on part of its 60-mile tour of some of the most breathtaking scenery in the country, crossing *forty-seven* bridges along the way.

To top it all off, there is an especially pretty waterfall in town, in an unlikely location. As the South Branch of the Root River bends past the southern environs of Lanesboro, it spills over a 150-year-old dam constructed of cut stone. The Lanesboro Townsite Company built the Lanesboro Power Dam to make a long, narrow lake. The lake was intended for sailing and similar pursuits to complement summer homes built on its shores. Today the dam changes the river into a gorgeous waterfall,

ROOT RIVER FALLS

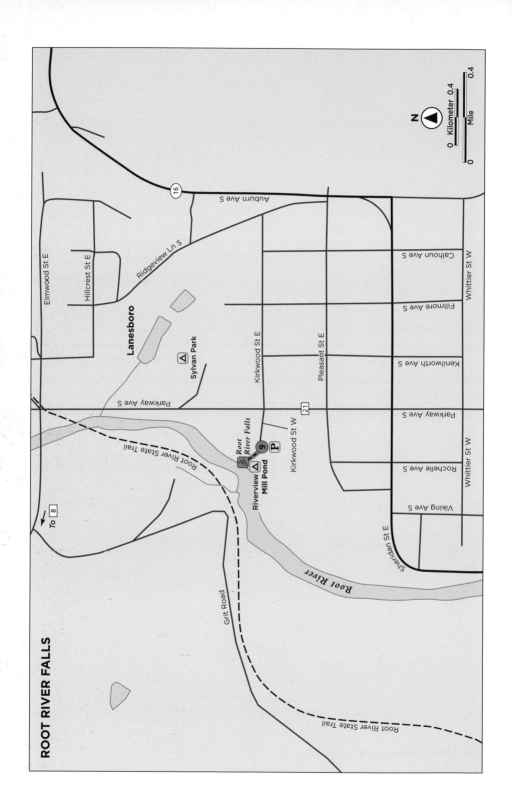

Root River Falls is a Lanesboro centerpiece. BRAYDEN MILLS

The Root River's bridal veil beauty. JIM HOFFMAN

with the cooperation of the water level. The dam is wide, spreading the falls into an elongated veil across the stone. Cracks and holes in the stone create tributary spouts of water that blend with the main free-falling sheets, and the falls appear as groups of hovering, gray ghosts. The river floats calm and wide below the dam, meandering on through town to join the Root's main channel continuing to the Mississippi.

The trip to the falls in this town is merely a sideline, however, with so many wonderful diversions close at hand. Lanesboro begs to be explored and is a picture-perfect town to roam about, enjoying the sights and sounds of the valley.

Miles and Directions

0.0   From Kirkwood Street, follow the path to the river. There are several vantage points in town, including a lofty view from the big bluff in town. Return to Kirkwood Street the same way.

0.1   Arrive at the crest of the falls.

0.2   Arrive at trailhead parking.

Lanesboro is known as the "Bed & Breakfast Capital of Minnesota," and is vibrant with many more year-round attractions. The drop-dead gorgeous setting is home to kayaking and tubing on the river, a lively arts and theater scene, unique shops and dining, and biking on the Root River Trail. Plan to linger awhile.

10 Niagara Falls

A trio of missing farm pigs in the early 1920s led to the discovery of this fascinating labyrinth of underground treasures and one of Minnesota's most unique waterfall experiences.

Waterway: Mysterious, unnamed underground stream
Waterfall beauty: 5
Distance: 0.8 mile out and back
Difficulty: Easy after descending the long and steep stairways to the bottom
Hiking time: Cave tour is 1 hour
Trail surface: Natural

Other trail users: None
Canine compatibility: No pets allowed
Land status: Privately owned
Fees and permits: Fee required
Maps: No trail map; USGS Harmony
Trail contacts: Niagara Cave, 29842 County 30, Harmony 55939, (507) 886-6606, niagaracave.com

Finding the trailhead: From Rochester, follow US 52 south to Harmony, then continue south on MN 139 to CR 30. Head west on CR 30 for 2.3 miles to the location. The cave and falls are accessed via the ranch house office.
Trailhead GPS: N44 20.799' / W93 09.885'

Note: Niagara Cave is open late May through early September.

The Hike

One of Minnesota's most unusual waterfalls flows underground in Niagara Cave, forming the centerpiece of tours through a spectacular labyrinth of limestone passageways. The passageways were formed by a combination of fractures in the large limestone formations and subsequent water erosion. The well-lighted tour through Niagara Cave twists and turns while traversing over 600 total steps. The tunnels are tall and wide enough to offer comfortable walking on broad, flat paths and boardwalks.

Descending these passageways, you encounter remarkable stalactite, stalagmite, and flowstone formations formed by the deposition of calcium carbonate and other minerals originally dissolved in water passing through and over the limestone bedrock. At several locations the passageways open into large rooms (one of which has been converted into an underground wedding chapel!), and fossils are visible embedded in the limestone walls. In the lowest reaches of the tour through the cave, a small stream enters the passageway, tumbling through a series of miniature rapids before disappearing beneath the artificial walkway and reappearing as the walkway enters an immense chamber with a domed ceiling 70 feet above. Here the stream emerges from immediately under the walkway and plunges 60 feet over a sheer cliff into a bowl-shaped cavern below. A viewing platform at the brink of the falls allows

Niagara Falls in its underground catacombs. NIAGARA CAVE

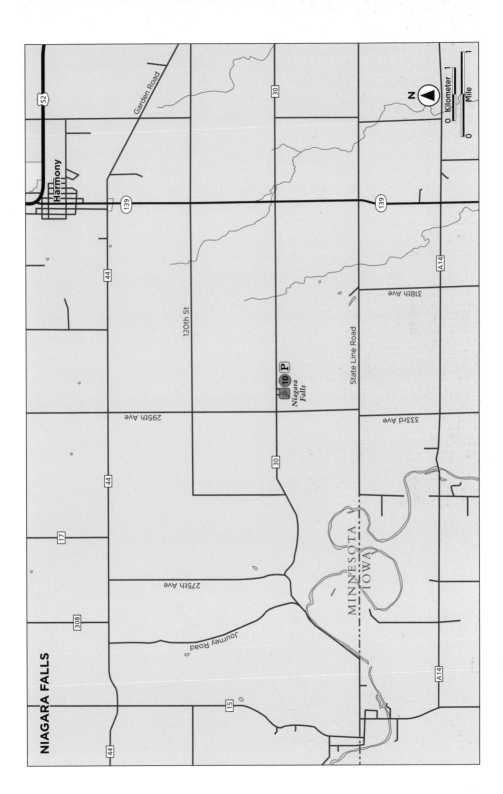

NIAGARA FALLS

a look up at the ceiling high above and down at the falls tumbling into the plunge pool far below. This is a truly unforgettable experience and a fantastic departure from exploring traditional waterfalls above the ground. The cave maintains a constant temperature of about 48 degrees F, and there is a long stairway to the cave floor. Come prepared with clothing and footwear to match conditions.

Niagara Cave is privately owned and operated and is open daily throughout the summer and on a more limited basis in spring and fall. The grounds around the cave entrance also offer a gift shop and picnic areas. The Harmony area is well-known for biking and cross-country skiing on more than 60 miles of the Minnesota State Trails system, as well as for its local Amish population. For another caving adventure, Forestville/Mystery Cave State Park is located less than 20 miles northwest amid lush, green bluff land and offers camping, hiking, horseback riding, trout fishing, a living-history exhibit highlighting the village of Forestville, and tours of Mystery Cave.

Miles and Directions

0.8 The 1-hour guided tour starts and finishes at the ranch house office for a total hike of roughly 0.8 mile.

Adventurous couples looking for a unique way to tie the knot can drop in to Niagara Cave's underground wedding chapel, site of several hundred subterranean ceremonies.

11 Pickwick Falls

This tiny, picturesque town nestled in Minnesota's bluff country is inspiration for calendar shots, history buffs, and romantics. Prepare to linger.

Waterway: Big Trout Creek
Waterfall beauty: 5
Distance: 0.4 mile out and back
Difficulty: Easy
Hiking time: About 10 minutes
Trail surface: Natural
Other trail users: None
Canine compatibility: Leashed pets allowed

Land status: Privately owned
Fees and permits: No fee required; optional mill tours available
Maps: USGS LaCrescent
Trail contacts: Pickwick Mill, 24813 CR 7, Winona 55987, (507) 457-0499, pickwickmill.org

Finding the trailhead: From Winona, follow US 61 southeast for 8 miles to CR 7. Go south on CR 7 for 2 miles to the town of Pickwick. The mill and waterfall are in plain view once in town.
Trailhead GPS: N43 58.834' / W91 29.761'

The Hike

Our waterfall tour takes us through dramatic rolling bluffs and forests making up the spectacular Driftless Area of southeastern Minnesota. Nestled in a fold in the hills above the Mississippi River Valley is the charming village of Pickwick. George Grant, one of the first settlers in this valley, took a look at the waterfall on Big Trout Creek and rightly surmised it would be a fine place for a mill. Grant enlisted help from his business partner, Wilson Davis, to construct a grist- and sawmill on the banks of the creek, using materials from the surrounding area. Limestone exhumed from nearby quarries formed the stately exterior of the six-story mill. Huge trees were sawn and notched to fit tightly together, creating the stately interior framework. Not a single nail was used to secure these great beams.

The mill began operation in 1858 and was a very busy merchant mill, producing more than one hundred barrels of flour every day. The grand, 20-foot waterwheel turned large millstones inside the mill to churn out the great quantities of flour, which were hauled first to the Mississippi River at the end of the Big Trout Creek valley. From there the goods traveled by rail or boat to the eastern states and beyond to Europe and South America. At the tail end of the nineteenth century, roller mills were introduced to the flour grinding process, and Pickwick moved forward with the newfangled machinery. The antique roller mills, flour dressers, and separators are on display today at the mill. After World War I the mill shifted gears and focused more of its efforts on feed milling, remaining in operation until 1978. In 1980 a violent flood roared through the valley and destroyed the dam and spillway, causing

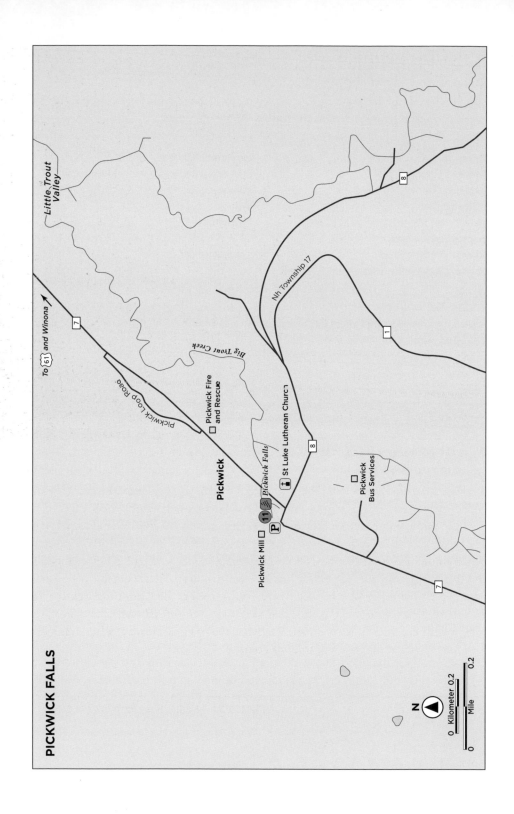

PICKWICK FALLS

Little Trout Valley

To 61 and Winona

Pickwick Loop Road

Pickwick

Pickwick Fire
and Rescue

Big Trout Creek

Pickwick Falls

Pickwick Mill

St Luke Lutheran Church

Pickwick
Bus Services

Nh Township 17

N

0 Kilometer 0.2

0 Mile 0.2

Pickwick Falls powered a busy 1800s merchant flour mill. BRAYDEN MILLS

significant damage to the mill. Plans to raze the mill were scrapped, and restoration efforts succeeded in bringing the mill back to its current historical brilliance.

The waterfall outside the mill is a lovely little tumble over a small, craggy limestone cliff. The trails leading down to creek level offer the best view of the mellow falls with the mill in the background. A small pond collects the creek below the falls and then slowly flows away from town between two giant bluffs covered with dense stands of hardwood forest. The valley road once served as the main thoroughfare for farmers pulling wagons to the mill, and the little burg of Pickwick was a bustling affair. Today the mill is listed on the National Register of Historic Places and is a wonderful destination on a trip to bluff country.

Miles and Directions

0.0 From the parking area, simply follow the trail to the waterfall. It is only a few hundred yards to the falls and back.

0.2 Arrive at the creek and waterfall.

0.4 Arrive at trailhead parking.

12 Little Cannon Falls

Small-town charm greets visitors at this reliably charming waterfall amid the mellow bustle of Cannon Falls.

Waterway: Little Cannon River
Waterfall beauty: 4
Distance: 0.4 mile out and back
Difficulty: Easy
Hiking time: About 10 minutes
Trail surface: Paved and natural
Other trail users: Cyclists and other users on paved trail

Canine compatibility: Leashed pets allowed
Land status: City park
Fees and permits: No fee required
Maps: Cannon Falls city map; USGS Cannon Falls
Trail contacts: Cannon Falls Chamber of Commerce, 103 4th St. N., Cannon Falls 55009, (507) 263-2289, www.cannonfalls.org

Finding the trailhead: From US 52 in Cannon Falls, exit at MN 19 and head east for 0.7 mile to the Cannon Valley Trail parking area on the left.
Trailhead GPS: N44 30.423' / W92 54.454'

The Hike

This pretty, multitiered waterfall is directly below Mill Street in Cannon Falls, at the end of the Little Cannon River's sojourn from spacious farmland near Nerstrand through rolling bluffs of Sogn Valley. Rolling, wooded hills and busy farmsteads surround this friendly town in southeastern Minnesota, and the scenic Cannon River valley winds through it for access to all sorts of outdoor-influenced fun.

The town has several nice parks scattered about, and Minnieska Park is one of the largest and most visited, due mostly to its location right next to this attractive waterfall on the Little Cannon River. Picnic areas and roomy blankets of grass are sprinkled throughout the park, and paved recreation paths connect to routes all around town, including the popular Cannon Valley Trail. There are great views of the waterfall from many different vantage points, and easy access for close examination. During low water, wade right out into the river and explore the falls with the soles of your feet, or stretch out on a flat-topped boulder.

The first drop of the falls is a 5-foot-wide, white grin of rapids stairstepping over boulders and flat rock ledges. After the main plunge the waterfall evolves into a gently sloping ramp of lively riffles, streaking the coffee-brown river with highlights of white. A thick pelt of tall trees crowns a stubby limestone cliff on the west bank, and grasses and other shrubbery poke up here and there on sandbars below the falls. The river rages in muddy torrents during spring melt and heavy rains, offering a whole new perspective on the generally placid stream, but it presents itself best through the summer and fall.

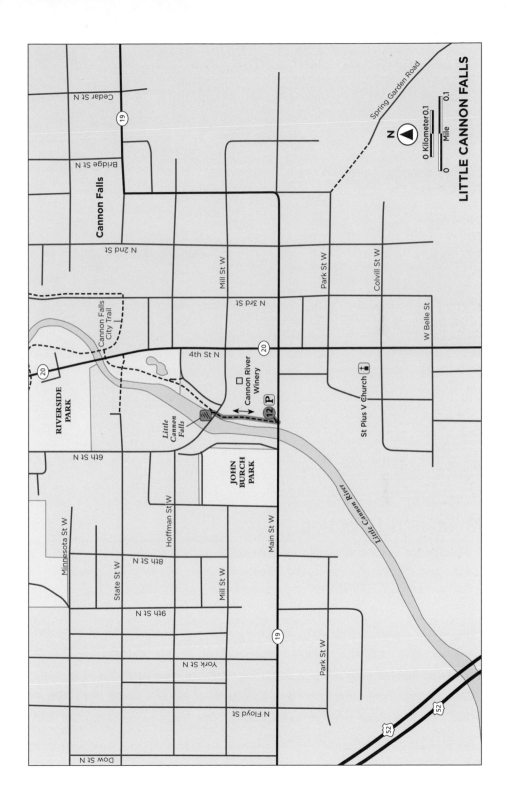

LITTLE CANNON FALLS

Cannon Falls

Spring Garden Road

N

0 Kilometer 0.1
Mile
0   0.1

Cedar St N

Bridge St N

19

N 2nd St

Mill St W

N 3rd St

Park St W

Colvill St W

W Belle St

Cannon Falls City Trail

20

20

4th St N

Cannon River Winery

RIVERSIDE PARK

Little Cannon Falls

6th St N

P

12

St Pius V Church

JOHN BURCH PARK

Minnesota St W

State St W

8th St N

Hoffman St W

9th St N

Mill St W

Main St W

Little Cannon River

York St N

N Floyd St

Park St W

Dow St N

19

52

52

Little Cannon Falls cascades brightly through its namesake town. BRAYDEN MILLS

Shortly after the waterfall, the Little Cannon blends with the Cannon River. The Cannon flows through a wonderful mosaic of high, wooded bluffs and patches of pastoral farmland to Red Wing and the Mississippi. Don't miss the fantastic Cannon Valley Trail, a distractingly scenic 20-mile recreation path following the river on a transformed railroad bed from Cannon Falls to Red Wing. Bring bikes, inline skates, or a good pair of walking shoes for a great day along the river.

Miles and Directions

0.0   From the trailhead, follow the paved path paralleling the river.

0.2   About 50 yards after passing under the road bridge, the falls are in view to your left.

0.4   Arrive back at the trailhead.

Fans of river running migrate every summer to Cannon Falls for the Cannon River's scenic home stretch to the Mississippi. From its namesake town, the river twists and turns through forested ravines and bluff land, with manageable rapids and abundant wildlife all the while. A local outfitter floats rafters down the 8-mile stretch to Miesville Ravine, or 13 miles to Welch, where ice cream awaits at The Trout Scream Cafe. Intrepid adventurers often make the 18-mile trip all the way to Ol' Miss.

13 Vermillion Falls

This boisterous waterfall causes a ruckus in its narrow and rugged gorge near downtown Hastings. Several locations from two town parks offer great views, including a gazebo shelter and bridge over the gorge.

Waterway: Vermillion River
Waterfall beauty: 4
Distance: 0.2 mile out and back
Difficulty: Easy
Hiking time: About 5 minutes
Trail surface: Paved and natural
Other trail users: None
Canine compatibility: Leashed pets allowed

Land status: City park
Fees and permits: No fee required
Maps: Hastings city park map; USGS Hastings
Trail contacts: City of Hastings, 101 4th St. E., Hastings 55033, (651) 480-2350, www.hastingsmn.gov/city-government/city-departments/parks-recreation

Finding the trailhead: Traveling southbound through Hastings on US 61, turn left just past the ConAgra Mill on 21st Street East. Vermillion Falls Park is on the left.
Trailhead GPS: N44 43.494' / W92 50.989'

The Hike

The Vermillion River flows lazily through sprawling suburbs, open fields of corn and soybeans, and past clusters of grain silos bordering hardworking farmsteads. The river whispers into Hastings, its current barely making a ripple, then suddenly comes to life in a thundering, frothy waterfall at the ConAgra Mill. The river roars over the crest and plunges nearly 50 feet to a deep pool at the bottom of a wooded gorge.

Hardy foliage grows in dapples of green from impossible locations on the gorge's vertical limestone walls, providing miniature habitats for birds and high-altitude feeding stations for bees and other airborne critters. This rugged chasm is a beautiful place, filled with thick woods of maple, ash, cottonwood, and cedar. The air is thick with the incense of trees and humidity of mist wafting from the falls. A large observation gazebo perched at the crest of the waterfall offers a great close-up view, and hidden trails in the woods along the bluff delve deeper into the gorge closer to the river.

A paved trail follows the gorge from Vermillion Falls Park into the woods and over a bridge above the river to Old Mill Park, site of the mid-1800s-era Ramsey Mill. Similar to the Pickwick Mill, the Ramsey Mill churned out one hundred barrels of flour per day until a fire in 1894 reduced the mill to ruins. The path to Old Mill Park also leads to Adams Park, Bull Frog Pond, and the rest of the city's 15-mile trail system looping around town. This is a great way to hike or bike to the best of Hastings, like the unique shops in the downtown district, or to a few of the more

The historic ConAgra Mill towers over the falls. BRAYDEN MILLS

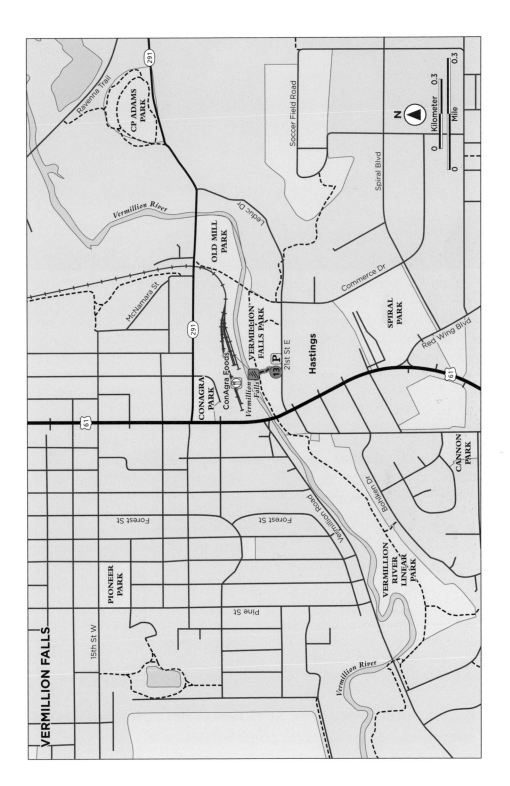

VERMILLION FALLS

Vermillion Falls thunders through a rugged gorge near two town parks. BRAYDEN MILLS

than sixty buildings on the National Register of Historic Places. Try apple or berry picking at area orchards, or treat your palate to award-winning wines at the Alexis Bailey Vineyard.

From the point of the waterfall, the river goes on to form the Vermillion River Bottoms, a magnificent archipelago of marshes, backwaters, floodplain forests, lakes, and islands. The braided stream forms a 17-mile-long by 2.5-mile-wide corridor of diverse natural treasures and wildlife habitat separating the Vermillion River from the Mississippi River. This large floodplain reaches from Hastings all the way to Red Wing, providing temporary storage for floodwaters from snowmelt and heavy rainfall. Over many thousands of years, the comings and goings of the water created the blend of aquatic and woodland communities we see today. This is home to a bounty of wildlife habitat, from lakes, streams, and marshland to forests and open sky. A small sampling of wildlife includes owls, kingfishers, dozens of songbird species, herons, and bald eagles. On the shores and in the forests are ducks and geese, beavers, river otters, foxes, raccoons, mink, and deer.

Miles and Directions

0.0 From the parking area, follow the path a few dozen steps to the gazebo overlooking the falls.

0.2 Arrive at the overlook above the waterfall. Simply retrace your tracks to return, or explore the neighboring trail over the gorge to Old Mill Park.

0.4 Arrive at trailhead parking.

Thousands of birds of myriad species use the Vermillion River Bottoms for rest and food during migration from summer breeding grounds to wintering areas.

Metro Area and Central Region

Here in Minnesota, we don't have skyscraping mountains, crashing ocean surf, or palm-lined boulevards. But we have lakes: 15,000 of them, and thousands of miles of rivers like nowhere else, near which we recreate with verve all year long. Pathways, pavilions, and open space filled with trails and teeming with wildlife complement the metro area's waterways. True to form, Minnesotans gravitate to them like little kids to a sledding hill. The Twin Cities and points immediately north reflect the same glacially influenced origin as the rest of the state, highlighted by water and gently rolling topography. Minneapolis and St. Paul are indeed twins in that they are geographically side by side and share a common bond in the Mississippi River, but they have distinctly different personalities. Minneapolis is often likened to a West Coast city, with its urban-artsy chic, action-packed nightlife, and glimmering office towers. The city's park system is legendary and a very visible and key cog in its character, as seen most every summer day in the active vibe around Lakes Calhoun and Harriet. St. Paul is more relaxed, cradled by bluffs and elegant, European-inspired historic districts, with an often quieter mood. Stately boulevards give way to miles of forested river frontage blending into a picturesque river harbor. Both cities, however, combine their characters to make this an award-winning place to call home. Each downtown boasts a vibrant arts scene, with renowned theaters, museums, and a stacked schedule of headliner performances. Also common to these two burgs is a rich, verdant landscape of woods and water, with places secret and well-known to glean the most of the state's outdoor vibe.

14 Hidden Falls

This little waterfall is secreted away in a cozy grotto of solitude and is especially handsome in the golden glow of autumn.

Waterway: Unnamed—waterfall is fed by an underground aquifer
Waterfall beauty: 3.5
Distance: 0.6 mile out and back
Difficulty: Easy
Hiking time: About 25 minutes
Trail surface: Natural
Other trail users: None
Canine compatibility: Leashed pets allowed

Land status: City park
Fees and permits: No fee required
Maps: Hidden Falls park map; USGS St. Paul West
Trail contacts: St Paul Parks and Recreation, 25 W. 4th St., Ste. 400, St Paul 55102, (651) 266-6400, www.stpaul.gov/departments/parks-recreation

Finding the trailhead: From MN 5 at the Mendota Bridge, head north across the Mississippi River. Exit on Mississippi River Boulevard and head north for 1.3 miles to the park entrance.
Trailhead GPS: N44 54.442' / W93 11.513'

The Hike

Hidden Falls Regional Park, part of St. Paul's park system since 1887, is a narrow ribbon of river flats, lowland, and dense woods along the shallow banks of the Mississippi River. Flanked by high, rugged bluffs on one side and Old Man River on the other, the park is a favorite for picnics, fishing, and bicycling or hiking the 7 miles of paved trails. There is also a maze of dirt footpaths sneaking through the woods, great for exploring and the chance to capture a little seclusion in the heart of a big city.

Concealed in one of the creases in the bluff at the park's northern entrance is the small waterfall after which the park is named. Easily reached by way of the grassy path adjacent to the picnic pavilion, Hidden Falls is a wonderful treat in St. Paul's grand parks system. Spring-fed from an immense underground aquifer, a small stream exits a portly circular drainage tunnel and spills onto a flat table of rock, pools briefly, and then gently falls past a high stack of horizontal layers of limestone. After its initial tumble, the stream stairsteps down two perfectly formed flights of flat rock to a second pool, tripping over a final 2-foot drop before winding away toward the Mississippi. Retaining walls built long ago with native stone line one side of the stream, and a craggy staircase follows the wall of the ravine up to street level. This is a pretty little waterfall with a tough, rocky exterior, and is a perfect venue to steal some peace and quiet from the parkway's bustle just over the top of the ravine.

After visiting the falls, explore a wonderful dirt footpath twisting north from the falls through the resilient trees and thick understory of the river flats. This area has

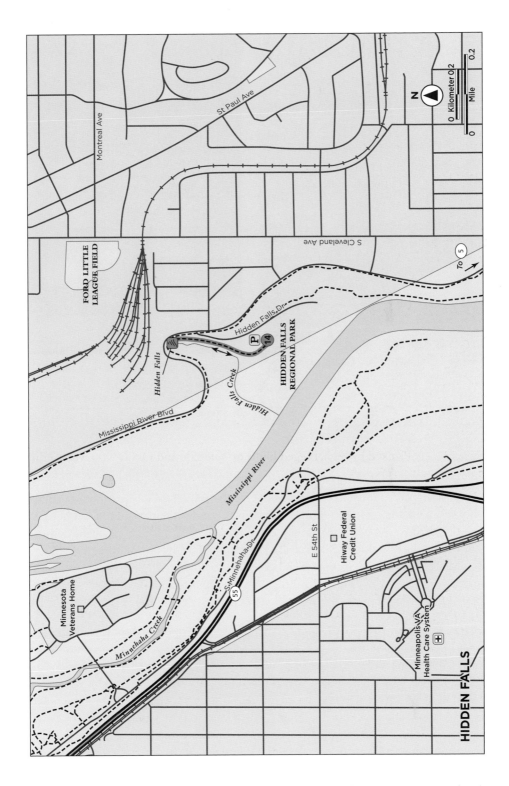

HIDDEN FALLS

Above: One of the metro area's prettiest waterfalls. Left: Hidden Falls slides over a ledge of layered limestone. BOTH PHOTOS BY BRAYDEN MILLS

seen spectacular inundations of Mississippi floodwaters over the years, but it always rebounds with a botanical vengeance. Paved pathways in the park in the southbound direction lead to the beautiful Crosby Farm Nature Area, another excellent destination and bonus to visiting Hidden Falls. The trails at Crosby wind through thick forest all the way to the I-35E bridge and continue to downtown St. Paul. Historic Fort Snelling stands sentinel on the blufftop on the opposite side of the river; tours are offered of the fort's compound and include fantastical tales of the area's younger days.

Miles and Directions

0.0 Follow the trail behind the pavilion through the woods to the narrow gorge and waterfall.

0.3 Arrive at the waterfall.

0.6 Arrive back at the trailhead.

15 Minnehaha Falls

One of the most visited destinations in the Twin Cities and a beloved hometown landmark, Minnehaha Falls delivers the scenic goods every time, backed up with storied Minnesota history.

Waterway: Minnehaha Creek
Waterfall beauty: 5
Distance: 0.4 mile out and back
Difficulty: Easy
Hiking time: About 15 minutes
Trail surface: Paved
Other trail users: None
Canine compatibility: Leashed pets allowed
Land status: City park

Fees and permits: No fee required
Maps: Minnehaha Falls park map;
USGS St. Paul West
Trail contacts: Minneapolis Parks and
Recreation, 2117 W. River Rd., Minneapolis
55411, (612) 230-6400, www.minneapolis
parks.org/parks__destinations/parks__lakes/
minnehaha_regional_park

Finding the trailhead: From Minneapolis, follow MN 55 south and east for 5 miles to East 46th Street. Turn left on East 46th to Minnehaha Avenue, and then right to the park.
Trailhead GPS: N44 54.928' / W93 12.609'

The Hike

Minneapolis is well known as the City of Lakes, and more than 150 parks make for an impressive list of locales for recreating in the great outdoors. Minnehaha Creek makes its leisurely, scenic tour of the city from Lake Minnetonka to the Mississippi River, showcasing some of the prettiest areas of town along the way. Dignified mansions and quaint cottages, secluded ponds and wetlands, and miles of wooded greenways are all on display. The creek concludes its journey in dramatic fashion at Minnehaha Regional Park, just upstream from the Mississippi. Camouflaged behind clusters of dense green foliage, Minnehaha Falls bursts through a slice in the vertical cliff walls and thunders 53 feet to a large pool below. It is a lively waterfall, announcing its arrival in a cacophony of frothy, vertical rapids echoing off the bluffs. A commons area perched at the edge of the bluff opposite the falls offers a postcard view, with a unique historical interpretive display of Henry Wadsworth Longfellow's "Song of Hiawatha" carved in the stone walkways and benches. This is a fine place to sit back in the sunshine next to the flowering shrubbery and listen to the muted roar of the falls. Just around the corner along the iron fence, a long, stone stairway gorge descends all the way down to creek level for close-up (and much louder) views of the waterfall. A dirt path follows the creek downstream and disappears into dense woods deeper in the park for more adventure.

Minnehaha Regional Park is one of the most popular parks in town, with over 500,000 visitors each year. The park's gorgeous location along the bluff above the

The city's celebrity waterfall. BRAYDEN MILLS

The big falls and verdant foliage. JIM HOFFMAN

Minnehaha Falls and its over the top pedestrian bridge. BRAYDEN MILLS

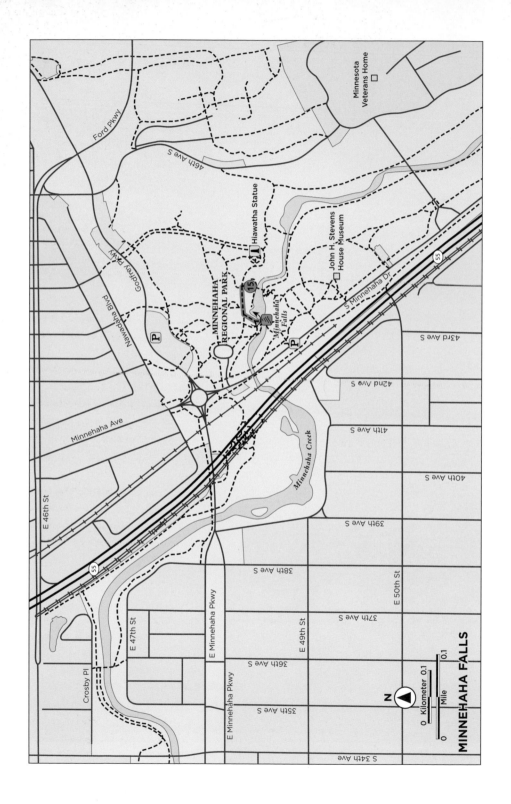

MINNEHAHA FALLS

MINNEHAHA REGIONAL PARK

Hiawatha Statue

John H. Stevens House Museum

Minnehaha Falls

Minnehaha Creek

Minnesota Veterans Home

Ford Pkwy

46th Ave S

Godfrey Pkwy

Nawadaha Blvd

Minnehaha Ave

E 46th St

E 47th St

Crosby Pl

E Minnehaha Pkwy

E Minnehaha Pkwy

35th Ave S

36th Ave S

37th Ave S

38th Ave S

39th Ave S

40th Ave S

41th Ave S

42nd Ave S

43rd Ave S

E 49th St

E 50th St

S 34th Ave

S Minnehaha Dr

55

55

15

N

0 Kilometer 0.1

0   Mile   0.1

Minnehaha Falls in full flight.
BRAYDEN MILLS

Icy teeth at Minnehaha Falls.
JIM HOFFMAN

Mississippi River offers an ample supply of majestic oak and maple trees on its grounds, lots of hiking and biking trails, and loads of history. The Longfellow House sits along the parkway above the falls; a beautiful two-thirds scale replica of Longfellow's Cambridge, Massachusetts, estate. This building was home to Minneapolis philanthropist Robert Jones, and was part of Jones's private botanical garden near the falls. Jones deeded his property to the city, and after his death his home was part of the city's public library through 1967. In 1994 the building was moved to its present location and renovated, and now serves as an information center near the former rail line. Also near the line is the Princess Depot, an 1870s Victorian-era depot that served nearly forty trains every day transporting passengers from the east side of the river to the uncharted west side.

The John H. Stevens House Museum is also an interesting historical landmark, located only a short distance south of the falls in the shadow of aged oak trees. The modest wood-frame dwelling, originally located near St. Anthony Falls, is believed to be the first home built west of the Mississippi. Many important events were discussed and decisions made inside this building. Hennepin County's first elections were held here, the city's name was proposed, and the county's boundaries drawn. Its present location was part of the Fort Snelling military reservation, and Col. John H. Stevens, considered the first settler in the city of Minneapolis, lived in the tiny building in exchange for providing ferry service on the river. Today the house includes displays of family life in the area, with tours offered in the summer months.

Miles and Directions

0.0 From the pavilion, follow the pathways to the commons area and overlook of the waterfall and adjacent stairways leading to creek level. There is also a bridge crossing the creek above the crest of the falls.

0.2 Arrive at overlook above the falls.

0.4 Arrive back at the pavilion area.

The 1800s saw crowds of tourists travel to Minnesota to see Minnehaha Falls, arriving in St. Paul on steamboats and boarding stagecoaches from there for the remaining journey to the waterfall and tours of the Twin Cities.

16 St. Anthony Falls

Steeped in state history and revered by the Dakota Indians, St. Anthony Falls gave rise to the flour milling market in Minneapolis and today still offers a splendid complement to the city's handsome skyline.

Waterway: Mississippi River
Waterfall beauty: 3
Distance: 0.5 mile out and back
Difficulty: Easy
Hiking time: About 20 minutes
Trail surface: Paved
Other trail users: Cyclists, skaters, walkers
Canine compatibility: Leashed pets allowed
Land status: City park

Fees and permits: No fee required
Maps: Minneapolis park maps;
USGS Minneapolis
Trail contacts: Mill Ruins Park,
130 Portland Ave. S., Minneapolis 55401
(612) 313-7793, www.minneapolisparks
.org/parks__destinations/parks__lakes/
mill_ruins_park

Finding the trailhead: The best view of the falls is from the Stone Arch Bridge. From the south, follow Portland Ave. S to its terminus at the river. From the north, follow 6th Ave. SE. Both routes lead to the bridge.
Trailhead GPS: N44 58.749' / W93 15.266'

The Hike

Minnesota has a long and storied history with St. Anthony Falls, the only significant waterfall on the entire Mississippi River. Visitors to the falls today enjoy a double-decker treat—the falls and the gorgeous Stone Arch Bridge.

When immense Glacial Lake Agassiz covered the land north of present-day Minneapolis, it created an equally impressive river from its southern outlet near Brown's Valley. The River Warren created today's Minnesota River Valley, and a huge waterfall formed on the river far to the south. The falls were not a permanent part of the landscape, however, and migrated upstream as glacial drift eroded. As the falls ebbed farther up the river valley, they decreased in size and diminished to mere rapids. A much tamer waterfall formed, dubbed St. Anthony Falls by Father Louis Hennepin in 1680, who is said to be the first European to witness the falls.

While the falls provided religious importance to Native Americans, white settlers soon harnessed the water's energy for their own benefit, using the flow to power a plethora of flour and lumber mills. Not surprisingly, overuse and large-scale erosion caused substantial damage to the waterfall. Poor attempts at repairing holes in dams and dikes only led to more holes appearing elsewhere. Logging companies upstream practically destroyed any semblance of the waterfall's former glory by floating 4.5 million board feet of lumber downriver. The US Army Corps of Engineers stepped in

Stone Arch Bridge. BRAYDEN MILLS

St. Anthony Falls and the Minneapolis skyline. BRAYDEN MILLS

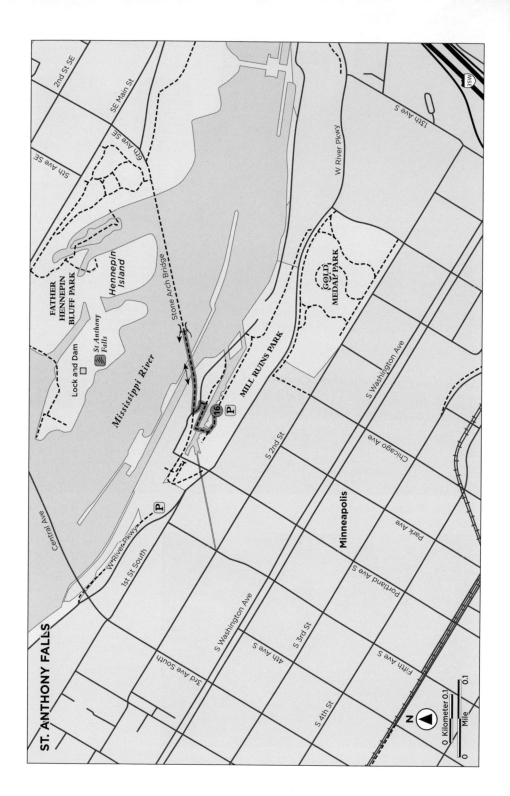

ST. ANTHONY FALLS

2nd St SE

SE Main St

5th Ave SE

6th Ave SE

FATHER
HENNEPIN
BLUFF PARK

Hennepin
Island

St Anthony
Falls

Lock and Dam

Stone Arch Bridge

Mississippi River

Central Ave

W River Pkwy

1st St South

P

P

16

MILL RUINS PARK

GOLD
MEDAL PARK

W River Pkwy

13th Ave S

35W

S Washington Ave

Chicago Ave

Park Ave

Portland Ave S

S 2nd St

Minneapolis

3rd Ave South

S Washington Ave

4th Ave S

3rd St

Fifth Ave S

S 2nd St

S 4th St

N

0 Kilometer 0.1

0 Mile 0.1

several times during the mayhem, and the bedraggled waterfall was finally transformed to its current uniform appearance on the shoulder of the Corps' lock and dam.

Although heavily modified over many years, St. Anthony Falls remains a handsome highlight to downtown and the inviting river's edge scene. Head out to the middle of the Stone Arch Bridge for the best view of the falls, where it slides in a long line over a concrete apron into a swift current of rapids. The Stone Arch Bridge itself is a wonderful historic landmark and bonus to the falls. Built by 1800s railroad tycoon James J. Hill, the bridge provided passage for passengers and products across the river. The bridge worked as a railroad viaduct until 1965 and is now a National Historic Landmark that connects museums, lively pubs, and dozens of restaurants on both sides of river. Check out the St. Anthony Falls Heritage Trail, as well, a 2-mile interpretive path with unforgettable sights and sounds of this city center gem.

Miles and Directions

0.0 From Mill Ruins Park, follow the path halfway across the Stone Arch Bridge for a great head-on view.

0.25 Reach turnaround point.

0.5 Arrive back at the park.

St. Anthony Falls was long held sacred by Dakota Indians who lived in and traveled the area. Native peoples believed the falls shared powers with gods and spirits, and the site became a central trade and lodging location among tribes.

17 Fairy Falls

Fairy Falls is another of those bashful waterfalls concealed from view unless you know it's there. Pay a visit and be treated to a fairy-tale grotto of rugged cliff walls and emerald green flora, beckoning with adventure.

Waterway: Silver Creek
Waterfall beauty: 5
Distance: 0.4 mile out and back
Difficulty: Difficult
Hiking time: About 20 minutes
Trail surface: Natural
Other trail users: None
Canine compatibility: Pets allowed, but keep them leashed near the steep gorge

Land status: National Park Service
Fees and permits: No fee required
Maps: Various Stillwater city maps; USGS Stillwater
Trail contacts: Greater Stillwater Chamber of Commerce, 200 Chestnut St. E., Stillwater 55082, (651) 439-4001, greaterstillwater chamber.com

Finding the trailhead: From the junction of MN 95 and MN 96 north of Stillwater, follow MN 96 west for about 0.1 mile to CR 11 (Boom Road). Turn right onto Fairy Falls Road and turn left up the hill to Orwell Avenue. Turnout parking is available on Orwell. Look for the footpath heading into the woods directly across from Orwell Avenue.
Trailhead GPS: N45 04.857' / W92 48.469'

The Hike

The steep bluff landscape of the St. Croix River valley exudes a comfortably rugged beauty, with hills of dense forest and dales of grassy meadows. Drifting the river in a canoe or traveling the scenic highway reveals grand views of this well-preserved slice of Minnesota. Hidden beneath a canopy of woods, tucked in the folds of the bluffs, are magical secrets not visible from the surface. Come, adventuresome spirits, and explore.

One of these secrets lies in a deep gorge at the northern fringe of Stillwater. Silver Creek winds a relaxing route through quiet fields and forests upstream, flowing almost in slow motion over the brim of the gorge. Fairy Falls whispers enchanting tales in delicate tendrils, falling gently between vertical flanks of corrugated rock to a deep pool below. Soft green moss, forever moist from the water's spray, colors the sandy-brown cliff walls in curtains of deep emerald green. A steep spur trail clambers down to creek level, past the imposing vertical mass of a colossal slab of rock making up one side of the gorge. Be careful here, but take just a few more steps to feel the mist from the falls. A shallow cave behind the water at the base of the falls provides a unique experience of seeing a waterfall from the inside. ***Note:*** Only approach the cave when water levels allow, and use extra caution to avoid taking a tumble.

Waterfall tendrils in a mossy gorge. BRAYDEN MILLS

The placid pool below the falls collects residual mist, and the creek continues its languid pace down to the St. Croix River. The gorge is a stunning, near-tropical place, thick with green foliage that allows sunlight only in faded rays filtered by thousands of fluttering leaves. Narrow dirt trails in the thick woods make for great exploring along the top of the gorge.

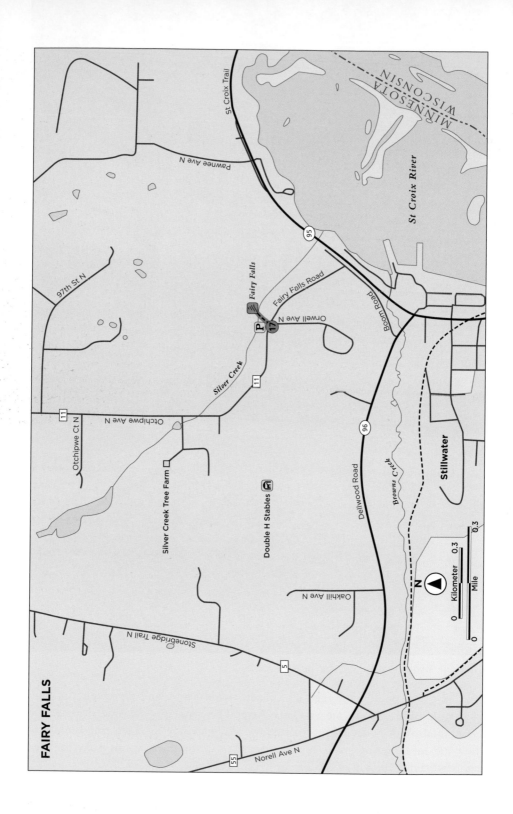

FAIRY FALLS

St Croix Trail

Pawnee Ave N

MINNESOTA
WISCONSIN

St Croix River

95

Fairy Falls

Fairy Falls Road

P 17

Orwell Ave N

Boom Road

97th St N

Silver Creek

11

Otchipwe Ave N

Otchipwe Ct N

11

96

Browns Creek

Silver Creek Tree Farm

Double H Stables

Dellwood Road

Stillwater

N

Oakhill Ave N

Kilometer   0   0.3
Mile   0   0.3

Stonebridge Trail N

5

Norell Ave N

55

Rail thin Fairy Falls. BRAYDEN MILLS

Explorations of another sort await just a short drive south in downtown Stillwater. A booming logging town in the late 1800s, with bragging rights of producing more lumber than any other place in the world, Stillwater also holds title to the "Birthplace of Minnesota." In a boardinghouse on Main Street, the Minnesota Territory was established as a state in 1849. The town blossomed as a tourism destination and today has one of Minnesota's prettiest and most popular Main Streets. Art stores, gift shops, antiques shops, one-of-a-kind restaurants, and a pedestrian-friendly environment make Stillwater a visitor favorite. The lift bridge across the St. Croix is a cherished city landmark, and the river itself provides recreation for boats of all sizes, and great fishing, too. The city also hosts festivals and other galas year-round, like the Rivertown Art Fair, Lumberjack Days, and a jazz festival.

Miles and Directions

0.0 From the trailhead, follow the footpath to a wooden bridge over the creek, right at the crest of the falls.

0.2 A spur trail descends the steep bluff to the base of the falls. Use caution here, but it's all sorts of fun exploring.

0.4 Arrive back at the trailhead.

18 Marine Mill Falls

Marine on St. Croix radiates charm from every street corner. With a pretty waterfall and hometown ice cream shop, plan to stay awhile.

Waterway: Old Mill Stream
Waterfall beauty: 3
Distance: 0.2 mile out and back
Difficulty: Easy
Hiking time: About 10 minutes
Trail surface: Paved and natural
Other trail users: None
Canine compatibility: Leashed pets allowed

Land status: Marine on St. Croix city property
Fees and permits: No fee required
Maps: Marine on St. Croix city map;
USGS Marine on St. Croix
Trail contacts: City of Marine on St. Croix,
121 Judd St., Marine on St. Croix 55047,
(651) 433-3636, marineonstcroix.org

Finding the trailhead: From Stillwater, follow MN 95 north 12 miles to Marine on St. Croix. Directly across from the Security State Bank building (120 Judd St.), the waterfall exits a half-moon tunnel under the street. Additional views are from the footpath in the adjacent woods.
Trailhead GPS: N45 11.840' / W92 46.111'

The Hike

Nestled in the folds of the western banks of the St. Croix River, Marine on St. Croix is an enchanting little hamlet with a firm grip on its proud history. Many town buildings still serve as originally intended and remain in impeccable condition along Judd Street. The one-block "downtown" boasts the 1872 Stone House Museum, Village Hall, and the Marine General Store. The Stone House is a beautifully rugged stone building constructed using techniques from Swedish pioneers. Inside are displays of articles from life in the village's younger years. The Village Hall is the oldest building in the state still used for government purposes. Way back in 1964, town residents had the vision to establish a restoration society to preserve buildings like these, and the community's character today is as strong as ever. A sizable portion of the village holds a proud position on the National Register of Historic Places.

This is also the site of the first commercial sawmill in Minnesota. Two lumbermen from Illinois traveled to the St. Croix River area and, attracted by majestic and plentiful pine forests, settled here. They built a sawmill with three mill wheels powered by the little stream nearby, and enjoyed much success in the logging industry for nearly sixty years. When the logging era ended, however, the small community met the same demise as the trees, falling into ruin and nearly disappearing. Today a signed interpretive trail and overlook in the woods adjacent to the stream's waterfall provide a look at the remains of the stone foundations of this mill and offer information on the village's history.

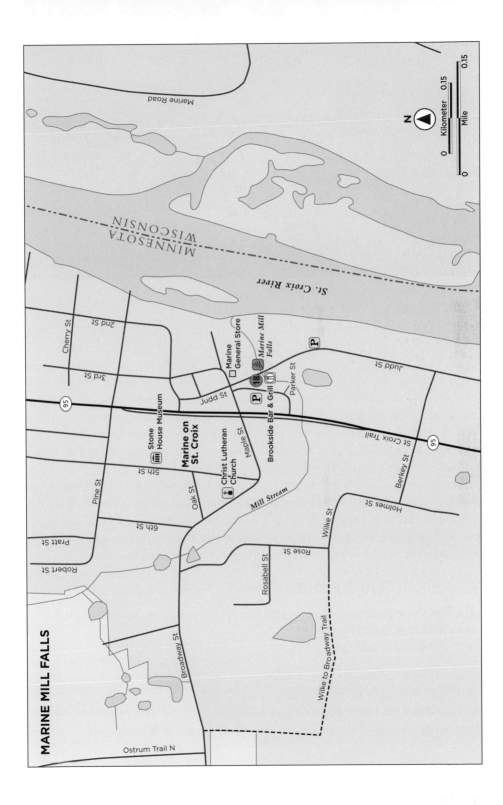

MARINE MILL FALLS

Ostrum Trail N

Robert St
Pratt St

Broadway St

Pine St
5th St
6th St

Stone House Museum

Marine on St. Croix

Oak St

Christ Lutheran Church

Rosabell St

Rose St

Mill Stream

Wilke St

Wilke to Broadway Trail

Maple St

Brookside Bar & Grill

Holmes St

Berkey St

St Croix Trail

95

Judd St

Parker St

P

Judd St

Marine General Store

Marine Mill Falls

18

P

Cherry St
3rd St
2nd St

St. Croix River

MINNESOTA
WISCONSIN

Marine Road

95

N

0   Kilometer   0.15
0   Mile   0.15

Marine Mill Falls below Judd Street. BRAYDEN MILLS

Area topography here is beautifully rolling with dense woods along the St. Croix, a National Wild and Scenic River. Many streams course through the trees in wide ravines and lush, narrow gorges. The spring-fed Mill Stream casually flows into town, briefly ducking out of sight and emerging from a half-moon tunnel beneath Judd Street in a vigorous cascade. Water spreads wide from the tunnel and stairsteps down a jumble of rocks to collect briefly in a quiet pool, concluding its journey with a short skip to the St. Croix. The view from the street above looks right over the crest of the falls, but the best look is through the trees on the high banks above the stream, accessed via several meandering footpaths.

Marine on St. Croix is a great place to lose track of time. Moseying through town with ice cream from the Village Scoop is the perfect activity on a lazy summer day, or you can sample hometown hospitality at the Brookside Bar and Grill, an eighty-year town favorite. The town's charm is infectious, and it's common to see people wandering about with big grins on their faces for no apparent reason.

Miles and Directions

0.0 From Judd Street, simply ogle the falls from the street, or wander the footpaths in the woods and around the old mill.

0.2 Arrive back at Judd Street.

In 1856, a ferry from the original village of Marine Mills busily transported townsfolk and tourists between the Minnesota and Wisconsin shores. A general store was built in 1870 to cater to those travelers, and the store is still a proud member of the community.

19 Curtain Falls—Interstate State Park

Get a two-fer at this state park on the St. Croix River near Taylors Falls. Walk among geologic ancients on the way to delicate Curtain Falls, and plan extra time for exploring.

Waterway: Unnamed creek
Waterfall beauty: 3
Distance: 1-mile lollipop loop
Difficulty: Moderate, with steep steps
Hiking time: About 45 minutes
Trail surface: Natural
Other trail users: None
Canine compatibility: Leashed pets allowed

Land status: State park
Fees and permits: Fee required
Maps: Interstate State Park map;
USGS St. Croix Dalles
Trail contacts: Interstate State Park,
307 Milltown Rd., Taylors Falls 55084,
(651) 465-5711, www.dnr.state.mn.us/state
_parks/interstate/index.html

Finding the trailhead: From Taylors Falls, drive 1.25 miles south on US 8 to the park office at the southern parking area. The trail begins at the park office.
Trailhead GPS: N45 23.613' / W92 42.127'
Note: This tiny waterfall depends entirely on snowmelt and adequate seasonal rains. During dry times of the year, it is common to see no water falling here. Plan your visit accordingly to see the waterfall at its scenic best.

The Hike

Already bestowed a place next to a National Scenic Riverway, Interstate State Park is brimming with age-old remnants of Minnesota's past. Full of holes, you might say. Near the river's edge at the northern entrance to the park is a collection of glacial potholes—ancient pockmarks formed in a maelstrom of sand and water from the racing rapids of the Glacial St. Croix River. One of these punctures in the earth is the Bottomless Pit, the world's deepest explored glacial pothole. Others include The Cauldron, Bake Oven, Lily Pond, and Baby Potholes. A self-guided interpretive hike through these primordial perforations is a great start to a day at this unique park. To reach this Swiss cheese section, follow the River Trail 1.25 miles north, or park in the northern lot and reverse the track.

Paralleling the dramatic cliffs of the St. Croix Dalles, the southern area of the park includes campgrounds, picnic areas, and river access for boats. Curtain Falls hides in the steep bluffs above. Head up the wide, well-maintained trail west from the park office and through a large tunnel beneath US 8. The trail rises gently past the decaying pilings of an abandoned railroad trestle, and then follows a steady upward climb on the Sandstone Bluffs Trail through deciduous, second-growth forest to the falls. Curtain Falls is a delicate trickle teetering over a small sandstone alcove, and dribbles

The Curtain Falls gorge. MINNESOTA DEPARTMENT OF NATURAL RESOURCES

even slower when moisture is limited. A trip in the spring or after a heavy rain rewards hikers with a pleasant look at this secretive gem tucked away in the woods. There is a fine view of the river valley's scenic splendor from the small overlook just below the crest of the falls, including a bird's-eye look at Wisconsin's Interstate State Park just across the river. Minnesota and Wisconsin formed the first interstate park in the nation in the late 1800s, in an effort to preserve the magnificent landscape.

Even when Curtain Falls is not at its peak flow, this short hike is worth the relatively easy walk. Around the falls, look for dark green blankets of moss adorning the moist walls, contrasting sharply with the orange-tan color of the bare rock. In spring, spectacular wildflower displays flank the Sandstone Bluffs Trail, including large beds of

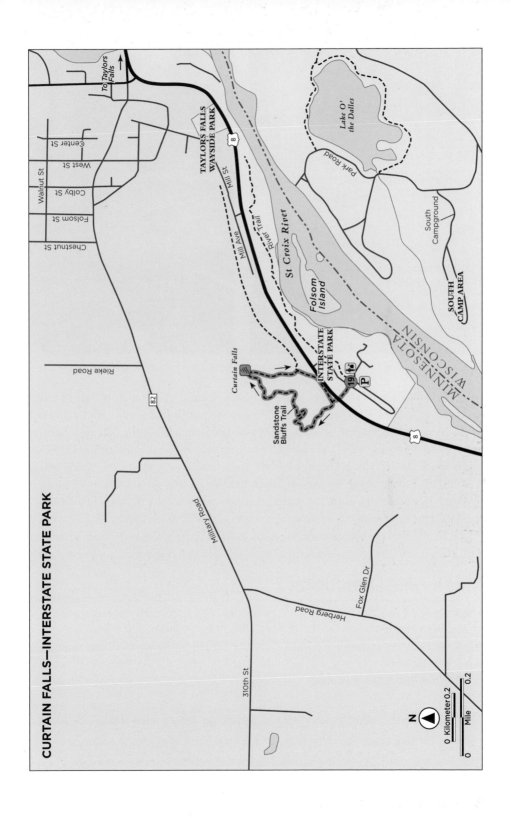

CURTAIN FALLS—INTERSTATE STATE PARK

Trail to Curtain Falls. BRAYDEN MILLS   *Stairway on the trail.* BRAYDEN MILLS

trout lily, trillium, wild geranium, and jack-in-the-pulpit. In summer, the moist ravine and leafy growth provide respite from the warm sun. And in fall, the yellows and reds of the forest provide a rainbow backdrop to the green and tan of the falls area. The trail continues for another 0.75 mile beyond Curtain Falls, looping through the sandstone bluffs above the river to an overlook high above before returning to the park office.

Curtain Falls and the Sandstone Bluffs Trail provide only a fraction of the recreational opportunities available within this park, which encompasses The Dalles of the St. Croix and includes both the Minnesota and Wisconsin shores of the St. Croix River. In addition to hiking trails, the park also offers camping and picnic areas, rock climbing, canoe rentals, and excursion boats that ply the rugged cliffs along the river.

Miles and Directions

0.0 From the park office, follow the trail through the huge tunnel under the highway to the Sandstone Bluffs Trail. The trail climbs steadily to the waterfall.

0.5 Arrive at Curtain Falls. Head south to the junction with the Railroad Trail, and turn right to the trailhead.

1.0 Arrive back at the trailhead.

The earth's crust cracked in the vicinity of present-day Taylors Falls, and lava oozed out, forming the dark basalt rock formations we see here. Much later, glacial meltwater carved the river valley, and fast-swirling sand and debris sculpted the potholes in the park.

20 Big Spring Falls and Wolf Creek Falls—Banning State Park

Bag two scenic waterfalls and take in legendary river rapids and great hiking at Banning State Park, a popular central Minnesota park.

Waterways: Wolf Creek and Kettle River
Waterfall beauty: 5
Distance: 1 mile out and back for Wolf Creek Falls; 0.2 mile out and back for Big Spring Falls
Difficulty: Moderate
Hiking time: About 45 minutes
Trail surface: Natural
Other trail users: None

Canine compatibility: Leashed pets allowed
Land status: State park
Fees and permits: Fee required
Maps: Banning State Park map; USGS Sandstone North, Sandstone South
Trail contacts: Banning State Park, PO Box 643, Sandstone 55072, (320) 245-2668, www.dnr.state.mn.us/state_parks/banning/index.html

Finding the trailhead: From I-35 north of the Twin Cities, take exit 195 for Sandstone. Follow MN 23 for 0.3 mile to MN 123 (Main Street). For Wolf Creek Falls, follow Main Street to 3rd Street and turn right. Head east for 0.3 mile to Old Wagon Road and the entrance to Robinson Park. Turn left to the park. To reach Big Spring Falls from Robinson Park, head past 3rd Street to Pine Avenue North and turn right. Head south (road becomes Pine Avenue South) for about 1 mile to a small parking area and trailhead. A park map is posted.
Trailhead GPS for Wolf Creek Falls: N46 07.961 / W92 51.466'
Trailhead GPS for Big Spring Falls: N46 06.812' / W92 51.770'

The Hike

Banning State Park is a long and skinny strip of green surrounding a curvy, 10-mile course of the Kettle River, one of Minnesota's Wild and Scenic Rivers. The river is a popular canoeing destination and is famous for some gnarly rapids with names like Dragons Tooth, Crusher, Power House, and Hells Gate. These whitewater playgrounds are some of the state's most challenging river runs, but portage trails bypass the maelstrom if you're in more of a take-it-easy frame of mind. Farther downstream is the site of the 1800s-era quarry that supplied sandstone rock for historical landmarks in Minnesota and Wisconsin. Five hundred stonecutters plied their sturdy skills at the quarry until 1894, when the devastating Great Hinkley Fire roared over the land, resulting in heavy losses for the stone company. The quarry closed in 1905. Many ruins of the former stone works are visible in the dense, second-growth forest along the river's western banks.

Wolf Creek meanders through the woods on the outskirts of the park, carving through crowded hardwood forest to its confluence with the Kettle River, just below

Big Spring Falls from the west riverbank. STEVE JOHNSON

the fury of Hells Gate. At the last minute before blending with the river, the creek flows through a secluded glen of deep green foliage and drapes over the sagging crest of a short, black rock platform. The water falls in a sheer white veil to a tranquil pool, surrounded by aged boulders with full beards of soggy green moss. Cloaks of clingy flora obscure the small cliff behind the waterfall and battle with the pull of the water to maintain purchase. The timeless passage of the falls has exposed streaks of rust-colored rock close to the pool, and huge ferns gaze with arched brows at their own reflections.

This place is mystical and seductive, where all sense of time seems to evaporate. Walk past fallen branches lying askew near the edge of the forest and look for the big, curvy boulder in the pool, the one with the front and center view of the falls. Settle in and let the soft touch of the falls massage your soul. Remember, though, that Wolf Creek changes moods rapidly with the seasons and times of fickle rainfall. If it is a dry time of year, this falls might be but a trickle of its usual handsome self.

Continuing downriver you reach Big Spring Falls, just south of Sandstone's quiet neighborhoods. From the trailhead on Pine Avenue, a narrow dirt path through a Sherwood Forest of dense foliage leads to an overlook of the falls. Along the way, look overhead to see a few of the 184 species of birds that live or vacation in the park. Near your feet might be a snake or toad or another of the nearly two dozen varieties of reptiles and amphibians. The trail passes through deep green fern gardens,

A hidden treasure at Banning State Park. JIM HOFFMAN

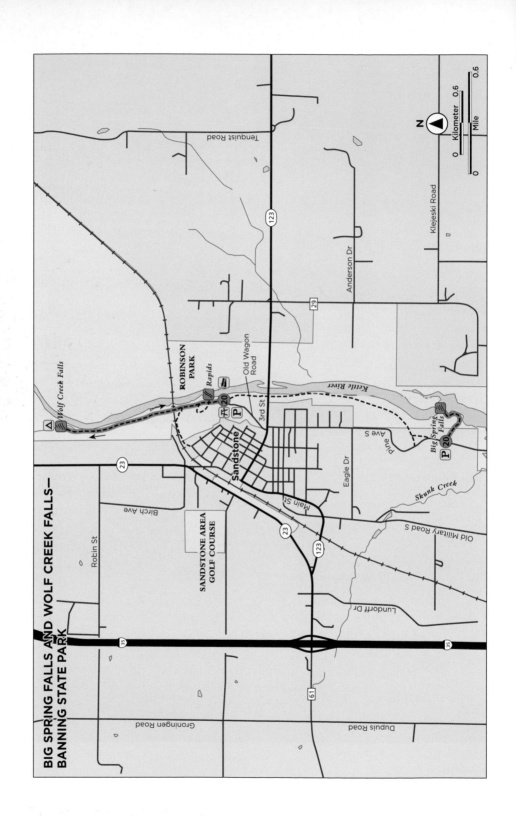

BIG SPRING FALLS AND WOLF CREEK FALLS—
BANNING STATE PARK

Wolf Creek Falls

ROBINSON PARK

Rapids

Old Wagon Road

Kettle River

Sandstone

SANDSTONE AREA GOLF COURSE

Birch Ave

Robin St

Tenquist Road

123

Anderson Dr

Klejeski Road

29

3rd St

Eagle Dr

Pine Ave S

Main St

Skunk Creek

Old Military Road S

Big Spring Falls

20

23

123

61

Lundorff Dr

Groningen Road

Dupuis Road

35

N

0   Kilometer   0.6

0   Mile   0.6

Big Spring Falls on the Kettle River. STEVE JOHNSON

a bountiful crop of raspberries and blueberries, and soaring branches of remnant Norway pine, white pine, and hardwood forest. Look into the trees for glimpses of white-tailed deer, foxes, black bears, ruffed grouse, and more of the robust animal life common to the area. Battleship-gray rock formations, mottled with white and pink and green splotches of lichen and moss, sprout from the ground. After a bend in the trail, a ledge of rock juts out between a couple of grizzled pines, providing an ideal place to view the river's activity below.

Big Spring is a gentle waterfall spreading nearly the entire span of an extra-wide section of the river. The "main" waterfall tumbles about 10 feet in the shadow of a huge table of horizontally stacked rock, with a single, stately pine tree perched on top. Two sidekick falls trip over the ledge adjacent to their larger sibling, and the whole works slows only briefly in a small, shallow pool before heading downstream. East of the big table rock is a wide and short waterfall, more of a lively rapids, that spills into a slow current around a sandy bend in the river, then makes a hard right turn over another 3-foot step, dropping perpendicular to the flow from the main waterfall. This collection of attractive falls may be small in stature, but there is much activity with the water darting in different directions, and the balcony view of the show is the best seat in the house.

Wolf Creek's fairy-tale grotto. STEVE JOHNSON

Miles and Directions

To Wolf Creek Falls:

0.0 Start from Robinson Park and head north through the woods.

0.2 Pass under a railroad bridge high above the river.

0.5 Arrive at Wolf Creek Falls. About face to return.

1.0 Arrive back at the trailhead.

Note: Past the railroad bridge, the trail shrinks to a skinny footpath paralleling the river. The path leads over jumbles of boulders and through tall grasses. Keep heading north to the mouth of Wolf Creek. The falls are about 150 yards upstream. A more civilized path to the falls starts from the state park campground.

To Big Spring Falls:

0.0 From the turnout parking area, hike the sandy trail southeast into the woods.

0.1 Arrive at the river. The waterfall is in sight upstream. Return the same way.

0.2 Arrive back at the trailhead.

The Kettle River is a state Wild and Scenic River, and the 10-mile section coursing through Banning State Park serves up some of the most challenging whitewater in Minnesota. The Class I to IV rapids are especially chaotic in spring, and visitors to the park can score riverside seats to watch the action. Whitewater rafting is also popular, catered by area outfitters.

Duluth Area

Heading north on I-35 at the crest of the hill near Spirit Mountain, the first view is invigorating. Lake Superior is the largest freshwater lake on the globe, with icy cold water reaching to a horizon way, way out there. The High Bridge crosses into Superior, to Wisconsin Point and driftwood and lakes filled with loon calls. The foreground holds the Aerial Lift Bridge, Canal Park, and Duluth.

Duluth is steeped in Great Lakes history and a present-day reputation as one of Minnesota's go-to places for weekend getaways, festivals, shopping, eating, and outdoor fun. The list of attractions is long and offers something for everyone, like touring along Skyline Parkway with big views from atop Enger Tower; hiking the city's wooded parks and deep gorges; shopping and dining downtown; or biking along the Lakewalk's rocky shores. There is enough to keep the whole family happy for many a weekend trip, in all seasons. As a bonus for outdoors lovers, Duluth is loaded with waterfalls, tumbling down through five scenic city parks. Only a short drive south, Jay Cooke State Park is a playground of hiking trails, camping, and the roiling St. Louis River with its dramatic waterfalls. In light of its proximity to Duluth, I included the Jay Cooke falls in this section.

Let's take a look.

21 Swinging Bridge Falls and St. Louis Falls–Jay Cooke State Park

This pair of beauteous waterfalls starts off any visit to Jay Cooke State Park with a scenic bang. See them both from the landmark swinging bridge, just steps from the visitor center.

Waterway: St. Louis River
Waterfall beauty: 4
Distance: 0.3 mile out and back
Difficulty: Easy
Hiking time: About 10 minutes
Trail surface: Natural
Other trail users: None
Canine compatibility: Leashed pets allowed

Land status: State park
Fees and permits: Fee required
Maps: Jay Cooke State Park map; USGS Esko
Trail contacts: Jay Cooke State Park, 780 Hwy. 210, Carlton 55718, (218) 673-7000, www.dnr.state.mn.us/state_parks/jay_cooke/index.html

Finding the trailhead: From I-35 southwest of Duluth, take the Carlton exit (MN 210) and head east for 3.8 miles to the park entrance. The falls are only steps from the parking area. **Trailhead GPS:** N46 369.262' / W92 22.260'

The Hike

Although not geographically on the North Shore, Jay Cooke State Park has all the ingredients of lands farther north.

After the St. Louis River journeys from expansive woods and wetlands northwest of Cloquet, it spends some slow time in Carlton's Thomson Reservoir and then meanders into Jay Cooke State Park. The root beer–brown water stirs along past some of the most breathtaking scenery in Minnesota, a fitting setting for the park's trio of waterfalls.

Jay Cooke's landscape boasts deep valleys and high ridges of dense northern forest, rugged rock formations, and high cliff walls along the river. Fifty miles of hiking trails squiggle through the park on both sides of the river, leading to all sorts of north woods discoveries. One of the main attractions, of course, is the river in its lively voyage eastward to Lake Superior. A short path from the visitor center leads to the park's popular swinging bridge, a stone and steel suspension bridge leading right over the river for great views of the action. Two falls are right here, both in sight from the springy deck of the bridge, and within even closer reach via trails along the river.

Swinging Bridge Falls is directly upstream from the bridge and always puts on a good show. Set against a backdrop of deep green—or blazing orange and yellow in the fall—this is a collection of a dozen or so smaller waterfalls and one biggie in

St. Louis Falls on approach from the south. STEVE JOHNSON

Swinging Bridge Falls enters the park in a flourish. STEVE JOHNSON

St. Louis Falls in a northern forest postcard scene. STEVE JOHNSON

the middle, all roiling past huge hunks of black diabase and greywacke rock leaning determinedly to the north. Look at the way these waterfalls shoot past the rocks at sharp angles to the main current. There is lots of foamy speed out there, too, as the falls blast between the rocks to hurry downstream. A trail along the northern banks of the river leads closer, but the terrain is dicey, and passage from solid ground to the rocks midstream is only possible when the river is running low.

St. Louis Falls is adjacent to the bridge, falling askew from the main channel. There is a nice view from the bridge, but head closer to get better acquainted. Across the bridge, hiking trails split off in a half dozen directions into the woods. Short social trails over the rocks close to the river take you to the top of a huge rock ledge with a fantastic view of the waterfall. Jagged jumbles of the park's trademark rock frame a group of cascading rapids falling over gentle 2- and 3-foot steps to a narrow cleft in the stone, where a larger 5-foot cataract plunges white and lacy into the mix. A small pool collects the spoils and aims for the main river channel beneath the suspension bridge. It's great fun to clamber on the rocks, even getting way out in the middle of the river to the big island of rock and pines across from the falls. Again a reminder: Keep an eye on the water and save your rock-hopping for times when the water is low. The river is very active in high water, with lots of different cascades foaming against huge boulders and slanted slabs of the ancient stone. A slip would hopefully just get you wet, but other scenarios include much less desirable ends. Enjoy carefully.

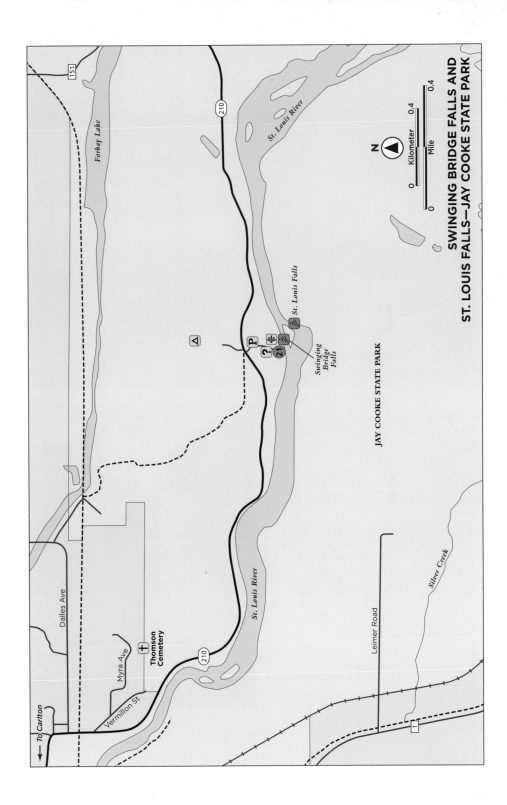

SWINGING BRIDGE FALLS AND
ST. LOUIS FALLS—JAY COOKE STATE PARK

Above: The St. Louis River downstream from the Swinging Bridge. Right: The park's landmark Swinging Bridge. BOTH PHOTOS BY STEVE JOHNSON

Miles and Directions

0.0 Simply walk from the visitor center parking area to the swinging bridge. View both falls from here or from trails on the opposite side.

0.3 Arrive back at the parking area.

22 Oldenburg Cascades– Jay Cooke State Park

This is a perennial go-to spot since my childhood, for rock-hopping and exploring on the lively St. Louis River. Postcard scenery comes standard.

Waterway: St. Louis River
Waterfall beauty: 5
Distance: 1.4 miles out and back
Difficulty: Difficult
Hiking time: About 1 hour
Trail surface: Natural
Other trail users: None
Canine compatibility: Leashed pets allowed

Land status: State park
Fees and permits: Fee required
Maps: Jay Cooke State Park; USGS Esko
Trail contacts: Jay Cooke State Park, 780 Hwy. 210, Carlton 55718, (218) 673-7000, www.dnr.state.mn.us/state_parks/jay_cooke/index.html

Finding the trailhead: From I-35 southwest of Duluth, take the Carlton exit (MN 210) and head east for 3.8 miles to the park entrance. From the entrance, continue east on MN 210 for 2.6 miles to the Oldenburg Point picnic area.
Trailhead GPS: N46 39.334' / W92 21.140'
Note: Only hike the trail when accessible. If the trail is closed because of damage or for construction, enjoy the view of the cascades from the overlook.

The Hike

Oldenburg Cascades are an all-time author favorite for feeling like a great explorer out on the wild river, jumping from rock ledge to boulder pile to islands of trees. Getting here requires passing the overlook way up on the ridge, and this is an industrial-size distraction from the river. Take a gander at the stunning views to the park's southern woods and a wide curve in the river just a short way downstream, flowing eastward to Lake Superior. Notice how the rock formations so common in other areas of the park abruptly end, leaving the river to coast along with nary a roadblock in sight. It appears the goings-on of very old glacial activity have left us with a mystery to decipher—something to contemplate on the way down the steep trail of natural stone and burly wood steps leading to the river and cascades. It is well worth the effort of climbing back the other direction for the close-up views of the violent surges and shouts of the river elbowing its way past an obstacle course of ancient stone.

These dramatic cascades begin as a wide shelf of rock, around 10 feet high and spanning nearly the entire width of the river. The St. Louis tumbles over this ridge in several different locations, sometimes trickling down in a respectable manner, other times jumping over in a raucous display of white foamy water tinged pale brown.

From here the river slides across a flatter ledge to the exciting stuff—hundreds of mini waterfalls dance around an orbit of boulders in the midst of the rapids. This giant assemblage of waterfalls forever shapes the personality and appearance of the valley. From the riverbank, it looks like an enormous root beer float tipped over upstream with its delicious ingredients spilling past this minefield of rocks. In spring

The cascades area is sliced with dozens of narrow chutes like this one. STEVE JOHNSON

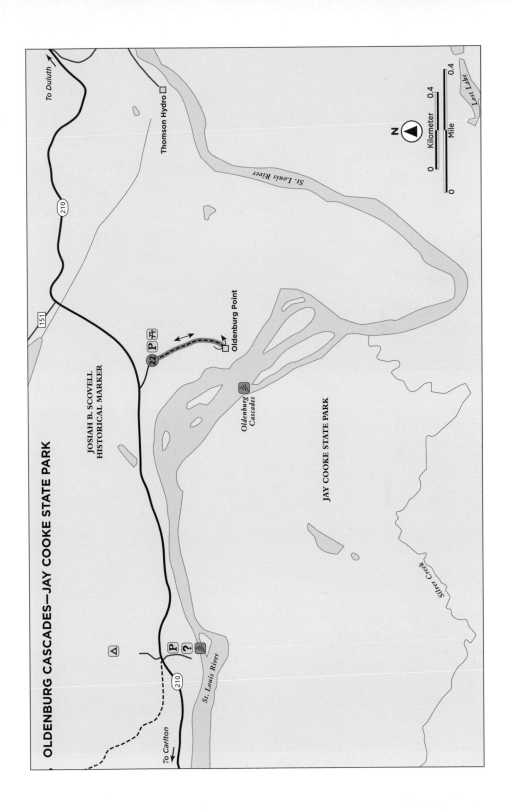

OLDENBURG CASCADES—JAY COOKE STATE PARK

JOSIAH B. SCOVELL
HISTORICAL MARKER

Oldenburg Point

Oldenburg
Cascades

JAY COOKE STATE PARK

St. Louis River

Thomson Hydro

To Duluth

210

151

To Carlton

St. Louis River

Silver Creek

Lost Lake

N

Kilometer   0.4

Mile

0   0.4

0

The main cascades roar over a ledge. (Check out the pile of suds in lower left!) STEVE JOHNSON

Great view of the cascades from the overlook. STEVE JOHNSON

A velvet smooth rock and tiny pool shaped through eons of watery construction. STEVE JOHNSON

Oldenburg Point trail. STEVE JOHNSON

and early summer, the thunder and mist from the cascades is beautifully humbling and best viewed from safe harbor in nearby woods. When the waters calm a bit, it is fascinating to look closer at the stony playground, peer into narrow crevasses in the rocks, and follow fingers of water through the labyrinth. Dozens of miniature rivers appear, staging their own flights through eons of creative landscaping.

Miles and Directions

0.0 From the parking area, hike out to the overlook for faraway views of the river valley.

0.4 Oldenburg Point overlook. From here, descend the steep trail to the river.

0.7 Arrive at the river.

1.4 Arrive back at the trailhead.

Inspiration to miles of backcountry splendor, Jay Cooke State Park's landmark swinging bridge is no stranger to the fury of the St. Louis River's tempestuous moods. High and roiling water in the summer of 1950 severely damaged the bridge, severing access to the park's southern reaches. The same fate invoked doom on the bridge in June 2012, when torrential rain urged the river into a frenzy, and its force sent much of the bridge downstream in pieces.

23 Kingsbury Creek Falls

Kingsbury Creek flows carefree from high above Duluth to a tour of the Lake Superior Zoo. Hike this short lollipop loop for the waterfalls, and then go see the monkeys.

Waterway: Kingsbury Creek
Waterfall beauty: 4+
Distance: 1.4-mile lollipop loop
Difficulty: Moderate+
Hiking time: About 1 hour
Trail surface: Natural
Other trail users: None

Canine compatibility: Leashed pets allowed
Land status: City park
Fees and permits: No fee required
Maps: USGS West Duluth
Trail contacts: City of Duluth Parks and Recreation, 411 W. 1st St., Duluth 55802, (218) 730-4300, www.duluthmn.gov/parks

Finding the trailhead: From I-35 in Duluth, take the Grand Avenue exit and head south for 1 mile to the zoo entrance. The trailhead is at the northwest corner of the lot.
Trailhead GPS: N46 43.549' / W92 11.4409'

The Hike

Kingsbury Creek wanders down the ridge from Mogie Lake up above Proctor. William Wallace Kingsbury was well known throughout Minnesota Territory in the 1850s. He spent plenty of time in the Duluth area and built a cabin along this creek. This well-maintained path today is a spur of the Superior Hiking Trail.

From the trailhead, hike through deep green and aromatic white pine woods. These are descendants of the towering, noble whites that grew here for hundreds of years before the logging boom. Hike the trail along a lazy U to a pair of cascading waterfalls. Cedar, pine, and hardwood forest line the boulder-strewn creek. A short way along the trail, a bridge crosses over the creek, with a lovely little waterfall dancing below curved pine branches.

The trail passes the Knowlton Creek junction, paralleling Kingsbury Creek and another short stretch of cascades, to a fork at the Old Thompson Hill Road trail. Take either direction to complete the loop, then return the same way to wrap up this wonderful walk in the woods.

Bridge crossing at Kingsbury Creek. CASSANDRA BALTES ▶

The creek drifts beneath an old stone bridge. CASSANDRA BALTES

Kingsbury Creek cascades through mixed forest. CASSANDRA BALTES

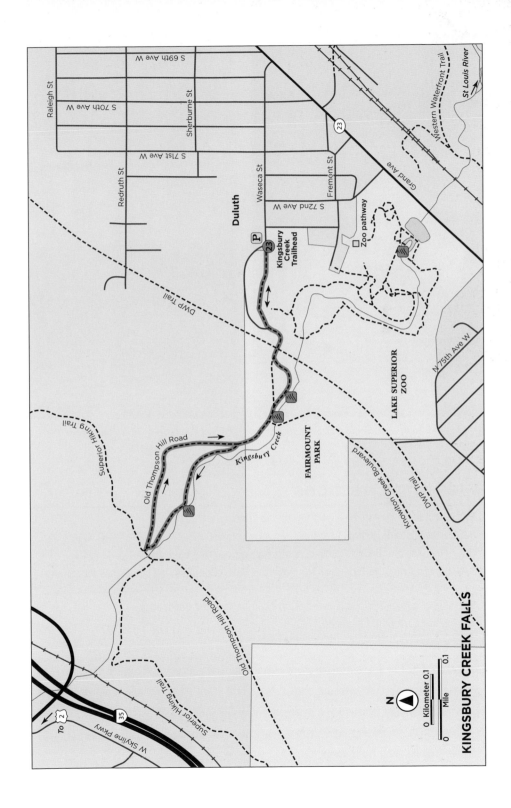

KINGSBURY CREEK FALLS

An old cedar with a great view of the falls.
CASSANDRA BALTES

A Superior Hiking Trail blaze leads the way. CASSANDRA BALTES

Miles and Directions

0.0 From the trailhead, hike west toward the creek.

0.1 Pass the DWP (old rail line) Trail.

0.2 First falls and bridge. Continue straight ahead, passing more cascades.

0.4 Junction with Old Thompson Hill Road trail. Take either fork; this route goes left, paralleling the creek.

0.7 Reach top of the loop. Circle right to head back to the trailhead.

1.4 Arrive back at the trailhead.

Founded in 1923 by a local businessman's inspiration from his pet white-tailed deer, the Lake Superior Zoo opened an elephant enclosure several years later and welcomed Bessie, the zoo's first elephant. Bessie had a penchant for ambling off zoo property and into adjacent neighborhoods, prompting more than a few calls from alarmed residents of an elephant strolling across their front lawns.

24 Falls of Miller Creek

Miller Creek is a relaxing stream flowing through Lincoln Park at the south end of Duluth. There are a half dozen cascades strewn along the creek and many places to sidle up and enjoy the sounds of the falls.

Waterway: Miller Creek
Waterfall beauty: 4
Distance: 0.8 mile out and back
Difficulty: Easy
Hiking time: About 20 minutes
Trail surface: Paved and natural
Other trail users: None
Canine compatibility: Leashed pets allowed

Land status: City park
Fees and permits: No fee required
Maps: City of Duluth park map;
USGS Duluth Heights
Trail contacts: City of Duluth Parks and
Recreation, 411 W. 1st St., Duluth 55802,
(218) 730-4300, www.duluthmn.gov/parks

Finding the trailhead: From I-35 in Duluth, take the 27th Avenue exit. Turn left and follow 27th Avenue for eight blocks to 3rd Street. Turn right and go one block to the park entrance on the left.
Trailhead GPS: N46 45.952' / W92 08.073'

The Hike

Duluth's park system boasts 129 municipal parks, playgrounds, and public places—lots of room to roam, to be sure. Best of all, several of these parks include scenic creeks flowing through heavily forested ravines that feel so isolated, it is difficult to believe you are in a big city. Lincoln Park was one of Duluth's first city parks and is home to a very busy stream.

Miller Creek's waterfall collection starts just inside the park entrance, where the creek cascades under a sturdy stone bridge and slides over a broad, flat stone bed. Halfway along, the water eddies in a rectangular-shaped pool perpendicular to the flow, shoots toward the north bank, and drops over a ledge to some smaller falls below. In places the falling water becomes trapped between wedges of rock, foams up, and spits out the nearest downstream exit. This is an active falls, with many side dramas playing out on a large stage. Farther downstream, the creek disappears in a dark tunnel beneath the stonework of the bridge at 3rd Street.

A park building adjacent to the crest of the falls holds community celebrations of various kinds and events for kids throughout the year. Simply stroll along the nearby path, following the south side of the creek, to the second waterfall, beneath the short cement bridge over the creek. This is only a 3-foot tumble, housed in a tight cleft of a small gorge, with a higher, 6-foot prelude falls above the bridge. The deep pool below the bridge is a popular swimming hole for those of thick skin and adventurous

Peaceful Miller Creek in the fall. JIM HOFFMAN

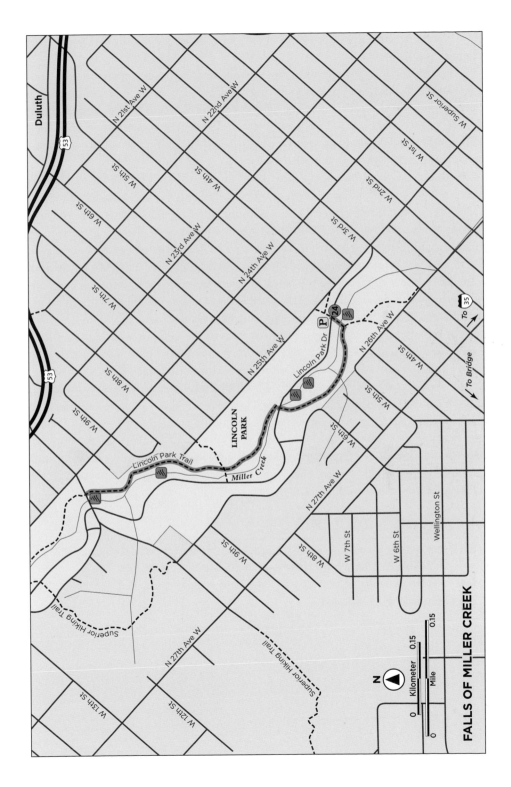

FALLS OF MILLER CREEK

mind. Watch how the creek sluices over the giant, smoothed slab of rock just before reaching the falls.

The park becomes progressively more primitive as you move upstream, and there is a wonderful trail in the woods following the creek. Up past the cement bridge at a gentle curve in the park road, veer onto the gravel footpath to the third waterfall. This is an easygoing cascade past mammoth boulders, tall cottonwoods, and dense hardwood foliage. A comfy grass terrace at creekside makes for a fine place to stretch out under a tree with a good book. Maybe a book on waterfalls, eh?

With the creek at your side, a short stroll up the wooded path leads to a cluster of 2- to 4-foot falls leaking through a jumble of fallen trees and boulder piles. This is a more hypnotic waterfall, its water echoing softly in the shaded glen. The trail continues up a steep hill to a footbridge spanning a steep-walled gorge flanked by thick curtains of trees and shrubbery. Look down for views of cascades above and below a narrow chute in the gorge. A short hike upstream from the gorge is a 10-foot waterfall on the south banks of the creek, adjacent from the park roadway. Leafy foliage obscures this one in summer, and there is no access to get closer without falling into the creek. Still, it is a handsome falls and worth a peek on the way up the road.

Continue upstream to the graceful stone arch of the 10th Street bridge. As Miller Creek flows through the arch, it slides over a huge slab of rock into a pretty cascade, gliding about 5 feet down to more level ground. Another tributary waterfall nearby shows its own style and grace, with a lovely backdrop of green through the massive half-moon opening in the bridge. Past 10th Street is one more waterfall, and Miller Creek dazzles once again, as the creek spills over a ledge below a footbridge in a heavy veil of white rapids set against the flat wall of a small cliff. A couple of huge boulders with conveniently leveled tops provide perfect seating for a relaxing interlude with the falls. Linger here awhile before retracing your steps back to the trailhead at the main park entrance.

Miles and Directions

0.0 From the first parking area inside the park entrance, view the first waterfall, then follow the Lincoln Park Trail along the creek, upstream, to the rest of the falls.

0.4 View the last waterfall just past 10th Street, then retrace the path to the trailhead.

0.8 Arrive back at the trailhead.

25 Falls of Chester Creek

Chester Park is a fairy tale you can walk right into, with an enchanting creek tumbling through a rugged gorge of mystery and adventure. This is a don't-miss gem in the heart of the city.

Waterway: Chester Creek
Waterfall beauty: 5
Distance: 0.4 mile out and back
Difficulty: Moderate (with some steep sections)
Hiking time: About 40 minutes
Trail surface: Stone steps and natural pathways
Other trail users: None

Canine compatibility: Leashed pets allowed
Land status: City park
Fees and permits: No fee required
Maps: City of Duluth park map; USGS Duluth Heights
Trail contacts: City of Duluth Parks and Recreation, 411 W. 1st St., Duluth 55802, (218) 730-4300, www.duluthmn.gov/parks

Finding the trailhead: From Superior Street in Duluth, follow 15th Avenue to its blend with Chester Park Drive. Continue on Chester Park Drive to the parking area for Chester Park. From the main parking area, follow the stone steps on either side of Skyline Parkway down to the creek and the trail. The waterfalls start here and continue downstream.
Trailhead GPS: N46 48.772' / W92 05.486'

The Hike

Another of Duluth's in-town hideaways is Chester Park. An author favorite from top to bottom, Chester is an enchanting place, revealing new secrets with each visit. Come along and let's explore.

The park proper is set high above town along the curvy scenery of Skyline Parkway. Picnic areas and a large playground for the youngsters are available here. Chester Creek parallels the park for a short distance before passing beneath Skyline Drive to a rugged ravine. Aged stone steps from Skyline descend to this heavily wooded gorge, where tall white pine, bulbous cedar, aspen, fir, birch, and other hardwoods team up with shorter shrubbery to wash the deep rock furrow in soft shades of green. The trail begins as a large platform of rock, smoothed by northern Minnesota's punishing weather and generations of visitors' footsteps. The rock slab extends into the creek bed and is likely just the crown of a colossal hunk of stone buried below the ground.

The first waterfall slides over one side of this rock in a wide, foamy veil, bordered on the creek's banks by huge pines and dense stands of hardwoods. Rock promontories dressed in green ferns and mosses with complements of purple and white wildflowers in spring stand tall above the creek. The whole setting is filled with refreshing smells of moist, vibrant flora. Only a dozen steps along the path lead

A three-pronged waterfall drapes over a huge mound of rocks. STACY DORN

to the second falls, a 4-foot tumble splitting around a huge rock island of ferns and miniature wetland pools, complete with cattails and waterbugs.

After only a brief flow past the rock island, the creek hurls headlong to the most dramatic of its waterfalls, and one with two distinct faces. Look to the south bank and the main chute of violent rapids blasting between monster-size boulders. Soaring cedar trees, anchored to the rock with clingy root tentacles, overlook the action. The north side of the falls is a decidedly different affair, as the creek glides over ragged rock outcrops in a lacy tumble of small flumes to an eddy pool below, where the churning water pivots back toward the main flow to another 15-foot drop.

Continue farther downstream to Chester's fourth waterfall. Two torrents race around gigantic boulders and plunge to a wide pool in a quiet glen of willow and aspen trees. The broad sandbar at the pool is an ideal hideaway to soak in the serene scene. Onward along the dirt path, beneath chickadee songs and complaining crows, cascades on the creek settle from the roaring upstream to a whispering mood, and the walk along this section is peaceful. Around a couple of turns in the trail, the gorge rises steeply and tall, with dense cover of pine, aspen, birch, willow, cedar, and lower shrubbery. A long, steep stairway leads up the northern side of the cliff to 17th Avenue, and at the base of the stairs a footbridge crosses the creek over this deep

FALLS OF CHESTER CREEK

N

0 Kilometer 0.2

0 Mile 0.2

Chester Bowl
Ski Area

CHESTER
PARK

Kenwood Ave

E Skyline Pkwy

E Skyline Pkwy

Rice Lake Road

N 24th Ave E

OLD MAIN PARK

E Kent Road

N 21st Ave E

Woodland Ave

W College St

E 8th St

N 19th Ave E

Chester Park Dr

N 15th Ave E

Chester Creek

25

London Road

E Superior St

E 1st St

E 2nd St

E 3rd St

E 4th St

Duluth

E 9th St

N 11th Ave E

N 10th Ave E

35

wedge of the gorge. Below the bridge is another waterfall, a narrow ribbon of foam and rapids, blasting through a slice in the rock to a deep plunge pool below. A smaller cascade struts a bit after the pool, and the creek moseys back to a gentle flow.

The last of Chester Creek's tumbling water emerges as the park exits its rugged confines into a broad, grassy delta, thick with hardwood forest and a web of hiking trails.

Chester Creek shows off waterfalls in different shapes and sizes. STACY DORN

Chester Creek tumbles beneath one of the park's stone bridges.
STACY DORN

Giant rocks allow easy access for an up-close look. The creek begins this upper waterfall in narrow forks of a cascading white slide adjacent to a small, mottled-gray cliff. A large plunge pool briefly roils about and then rushes off to a resounding duel of two higher falls in the shadow of the masterfully crafted stone bridge at 4th Street. The northern contender spouts a graceful rooster tail of white, while a mammoth boulder in colorful armor of pink and green lichen and drapes of mossy grass provides a solid defense. To the south, the creek funnels into a foxhole between the brawn of two weathered gray rock escorts, free-falling 4 feet to a hasty slide to mingle with its flanking counterpart. Now allies, the waters of the falls flow into the blackness of an aged arched tunnel through the sheer, ivy-laced wall of the bridge, in a final advance to Lake Superior.

Miles and Directions

0.0   From the trailhead, descend to the trails along the creek and explore downstream and back upstream.

0.2   Turnaround point at East 4th Street.

0.4   Arrive back at the trailhead.

Just upstream from the waterfalls area is Duluth's popular Chester Bowl alpine ski and recreation area. A local favorite for hitting the slopes, Chester also hosts all sorts of concerts and year-round outdoor adventures and a lively winter carnival. See www.chesterbowl.org for more information.

26 Falls of Tischer Creek

Tischer Creek is overflowing with waterfalls in one of Duluth's prettiest areas. Congdon Park is a small, skinny park in a deep gorge of red cliffs, dense stands of cedar, slender dirt footpaths, and bridges over the creek. It is an absolutely gorgeous trek and a perfect place to disappear for a few hours.

Waterway: Tischer Creek
Waterfall beauty: 5
Distance: 1.2-mile loop
Difficulty: Easy
Hiking time: About 50 minutes
Trail surface: Stone steps and natural pathways
Other trail users: None

Canine compatibility: Leashed pets allowed
Land status: City park
Fees and permits: No fee required
Maps: City of Duluth park map; USGS Duluth Heights
Trail contacts: City of Duluth Parks and Recreation, 411 W. 1st St., Duluth 55802, (218) 730-4300, www.duluthmn.gov/parks

Finding the trailhead: From London Road (MN 61) in Duluth, follow 32nd Avenue North to its junction with Congdon Park Drive. At East 1st Street, turn right to reach the creek. Follow the craggy stone steps down to the creekside trail.
Trailhead GPS: N46 49.097' / W92 03.408'

The Hike

Congdon Park is named after Chester Congdon, the prominent Duluth businessman whose early 1900s estate, the Glensheen Mansion, is one of the city's most popular destinations.

Your waterfall tour starts in a canopy of thick woods right below East 1st Street, on the dirt trail next to the creek. Stroll along this scenic trail for a short while to the second footbridge, and listen to the siren song of Wildflower Falls, a rail-thin waterfall situated at a right angle to the creek. Named for the colorful display of tiny purple and pink and white flowers decorating the crest of the falls in spring, this pretty ribbon of lace pours gently over the red cliff on the opposite side of the gorge, meeting the creek in little splashes. The top of the ridge is resplendent in bright white birch and shimmering aspen, and above your head, on the trail side of the gorge, are clusters of robust cedars and white pine. The trip has barely begun, and it is already difficult to leave this scene.

Around a couple of gentle bends is the second helping: a long, three-tiered falls with a soaring cliff of red rock on one side and dense pine woods opposite. The creek rushes beneath another metal rail bridge, emptying into a calm, deep pool. A flight of cement steps climbs to the higher elevation of the creek at the crest of this cascade. This is a great vantage point to see the creek fall toward the bridge, make a hard left turn, and vanish downstream. A soft coat of moss and lichen swaddles the cliff walls on this upper part of the waterfall. Farther ahead is Redcliff Falls, descending from a place far up the gorge. This falls is a long cascade of white, flowing like a wedding dress train and just as captivating. High, red rock walls tilt steeply away from the falls on the north side, and a pile of boulders makes a solid wall on the southern banks. The setting is especially beautiful, and several handy boulders in the creek make great lounge chairs for extended lingering.

Head up the stone steps; only a short hike farther upstream is White Falls, a skinny chute of whitewater funneling through a notch in craggy rock formations. The tributary waterfall to the left trickles down into an alcove, and the two meet in a small pool, tripping over a couple of smaller cascades below. It is another mystical venue of reflection and relaxation. Just past 4th Street is Table Rock Falls, a rapids sliding over a huge, inclined tabletop rock. This waterfall seems to appear out of nowhere from its concealed locale behind thick hardwood foliage. A leaning tree reaches long, gnarled fingers over the waterfall and the spinning pool at its base.

Upstream is Tischer's sixth waterfall (or the first one, if you start the trail from this end of the park). This is a real beauty, nestled among a mix of pine, willow, alder, and

Tischer Creek gorge and trail bridge. JIM HOFFMAN

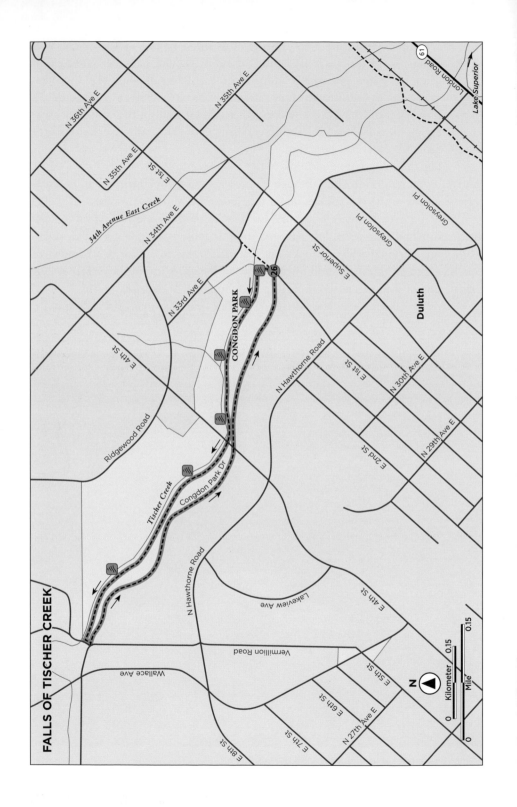

FALLS OF TISCHER CREEK

CONGDON PARK

Duluth

Tischer Creek

34th Avenue East Creek

Congdon Park Dr

N 36th Ave E

N 35th Ave E

N 35th Ave E

E 1st St

N 34th Ave E

N 33rd Ave E

E 4th St

Ridgewood Road

N Hawthorne Road

N Hawthorne Road

Wallace Ave

Vermillion Road

Lakeview Ave

E 2nd St

E 1st St

E 4th St

E 5th St

E 6th St

E 7th St

E 8th St

N 27th Ave E

N 29th Ave E

N 30th Ave E

E Superior St

Greysolon Pl

Greysolon Pl

London Road

Lake Superior

61

26

N

Kilometer   0.15

Mile   0.15

0

0

maple. The creek dances over a dozen steps in a lively liquid boogie between square-edged boulders and a pint-size rock island. It's a very pretty falls in a rugged environ of rock and woods, and a fine concluding act to this short exploration of Congdon Park. Vermillion Road marks the end of the trail today. An about-face allows a leisurely return trip on the gray gravel path above the creek gorge.

Miles and Directions

0.0 From the trailhead, descend the steps to the creek and follow the trail upstream to view the various falls.

0.2 Junction with 4th Street. Continue along the creek.

0.5 At Vermillion Road, follow the path to the upper trail to return along Congdon Park Drive.

1.2 Arrive back at the trailhead.

The Glensheen Mansion in Duluth is Minnesota's most visited historic home. The 39-room manse was built by the influential Congdon family beginning in 1905. The Congdons spearheaded iron ore mining in northern Minnesota and preservation of area lands for public use, including their namesake park in Duluth. Tours of the mansion and grounds are available year-round.

27 Falls of Amity Creek—Amity and Lester Parks

Amity Creek flows through one of the most distractingly beautiful areas of Duluth, touching two scenic parks along the way and showing off a collection of lively waterfalls.

Waterway: Amity Creek
Waterfall beauty: 4
Distance: 0.8 mile out and back for the first waterfall; 0.1 mile for the second and third falls
Difficulty: Easy
Hiking time: About 50 minutes
Trail surface: Stone steps and natural pathways

Other trail users: None
Canine compatibility: Leashed pets allowed
Land status: City park
Fees and permits: No fee required
Maps: City of Duluth park map; USGS Duluth Heights
Trail contacts: City of Duluth Parks and Recreation, 411 W. 1st St., Duluth 55802, (218) 730-4300, www.duluthmn.gov/parks

Finding the trailhead: From London Road, follow North 60th Avenue north to East Superior Street. Turn right. After two blocks, turn left on Occidental Boulevard. Park in the turnout. Follow the rustic path above the creek. The second waterfall is 0.4 mile north on Seven Bridges Road. Bike or drive to the bridge. View the falls from the bridge or social trails. For the third waterfall, follow Seven Bridges Road 0.9 mile to a turnout on the east side of the road. Follow the trails to the river.
Trailhead GPS: N46 50 340' / W92 00.459'

The Hike

Amity Creek flows from Antoinette Lake over Duluth's highest reaches and through stunning scenery of hardwood forest and sentinel pines to a last-minute rendezvous with the Lester River before sliding into Lake Superior. Technically considered a branch of the Lester, Amity has a personality all its own, and shows off three handsome waterfalls along the way.

The hike explores Amity's falls from bottom to top, with a mix of hiking and driving or cycling, starting from the idyllic neighborhood along Occidental Boulevard, just above Superior Street. A stately pine forest sets the stage for the trip upstream, and just shy of 0.5 mile along the dirt path is the first waterfall. Amity Falls, also known as The Deeps, is the main attraction. A gazebo perched within splashing distance from the rushing creek is a wonderful place to while away some time, and the wood-rail footbridge crossing to the northern side of the gorge provides an

Amity Creek at The Deeps. STACY DORN ▶

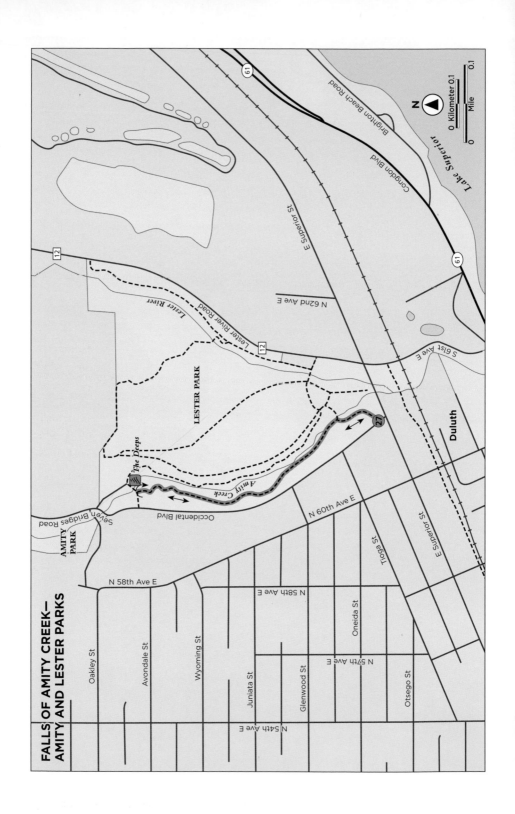

FALLS OF AMITY CREEK—
AMITY AND LESTER PARKS

AMITY PARK

Seven Bridges Road

The Deeps

LESTER PARK

Lester River

Lester River Road

N 58th Ave E

Oakley St

Avondale St

Wyoming St

Juniata St

Glenwood St

Otsego St

N 54th Ave E

N 57th Ave E

N 58th Ave E

Tioga St

Oneida St

N 60th Ave E

Occidental Blvd

Amity Creek

27

Duluth

E Superior St

S 61st Ave E

N 62nd Ave E

E Superior St

Congdon Blvd

Brighton Beach Road

Lake Superior

12

12

61

61

N

0 Kilometer 0.1

0   0.1
Mile

elevated view of the waterfall as it plummets out of sight. The creek is often a torrent of whitewater, especially in the spring, but it calms down to a more neighborly pace later in the year. A steep cliff rises on both sides, but there is easy access to the creek below the falls via stairstep rocks from the bridge. The deep pool here is irresistible to the young and brave; locals can be found flinging themselves off the high rock ledges on the other side of the creek into the frigid waters.

The next waterfall is a few turns along Seven Bridges Road, a lovely passage through the scenic highlands of Duluth, with numerous creek crossings over magnificent stone-crafted bridges. Just before reaching the first bridge is our next waterfall; get the best look at this one from right up on the road. A gap in the trees allows a look straight down at a four-fingered waterfall, commencing after a sharp bend in the creek. A cascade of rapids forms above and then spreads into four distinct chutes of white, with the middle one closing behind a huge boulder just before the base of the falls. In higher water, the creek streams past in three chutes, and it looks like a giant trident. A path is available, dropping steeply into the woods and down to the falls way below.

At the sixth bridge is another exciting waterfall, and another popular swimming hole. Park in the turnout before the bridge and follow the short trails to the creek. Above the bridge, beginning up near Skyline Parkway, is a long stairway cascade, skipping over five separate ledges before reaching the stone bridge. Past the bridge's arch, the creek zigs right and then zags left to an easy slide into a large, deep pool circled by a coliseum of gigantic, gray-black boulders. This pool is a favorite cooling-off destination in Duluth's short summer season. Below the pool the creek slides over another gentle cascade, eddies briefly, and finally meets calm water at a distant bend downstream.

Miles and Directions

0.0 From the creek's lower section at Superior Street, take the scenic route and follow the rustic path along the creek to the falls. Plan B is to head up Occidental Boulevard to the top of the hill to the crest of the falls. A stone stairway descends to creek level.

0.4 Arrive at the bridge above first waterfall.

0.8 Arrive back at the Superior Street trailhead.

Option: Continue up Seven Bridges Road to view the other falls.

28 Falls of Lester River–Lester Park

The Lester River is the northernmost river in Duluth proper, and like its brethren to the south, offers multiple waterfalls to enjoy.

Waterway: Lester River
Waterfall beauty: 3–4
Distance: 0.6 mile out and back
Difficulty: Easy to moderate
Hiking time: About 40 minutes
Trail surface: Stone steps and natural pathways
Other trail users: None

Canine compatibility: Leashed pets allowed
Land status: City park
Fees and permits: No fee required
Maps: City of Duluth park map; USGS Duluth Heights
Trail contacts: City of Duluth Parks and Recreation, 411 W. 1st St., Duluth 55802, (218) 730-4300, www.duluthmn.gov/parks

Finding the trailhead: The lower trailhead is at the junction of 61st Avenue East and East Superior Street in Duluth.
Trailhead GPS: N46 50.353' / W92 00.368'

The Hike

Your exploration of the Lester River starts close to Lake Superior and heads upstream to more remote settings. The first waterfall on the list is Japp Hole, right under the Superior Street bridge. Dirt paths lead through a copse of woods to a couple of different views of this urban waterfall, adjacent to a railroad bridge frequented by sightseeing train tours. Japp Hole is a deceptively attractive falls, tumbling over seven different drops to a larger, 20-foot free fall to the base of the cliff. The steep-walled gorge is narrow at the falls and morphs into a nice wooded canyon, colored pine green, as the smooth waters drift into the lake.

The next pair of waterfalls drop on either side of the park bridge leading to the picnic areas and the ski and hiking trails. The downstream falls zips through a chute of raggedy rocks and spreads to a fan of rapids below. The upstream falls is a short hike from the park bridge. Follow the path adjacent to the parking area about 50 yards upstream. The waterfall is visible through some wispy foliage and via trails to the river's edge, or from the park bridge. This petite, 3-foot falls, bordered by tall cedars and pines, is composed of four distinct chutes, each falling into a wide, shallow pool and then drifting down to the bridge. There is easy access from the parking area along the dirt path paralleling the river, and even in such close proximity to the heavily visited park, it is often a quiet and relaxing place.

The path from the parking area leads to Lester Falls through a scenic woods of huge pines, with the river as hiking partner. There is also a small turnout just before the entrance to the golf course on Lester River Road. Check out a great view of the

An aged stone bridge watches over the Lester River. STACY DORN

crest of this waterfall from the trail high above the falls, or follow the post-and-cable railing to a rustic path down to the water's level for a closer look. The path descends rugged stone steps to the river's edge and an open "beach" of small river rock. Do you hear thunder? Indeed, Lester Falls announces itself before you see it, and just a short way along the river you are treated to a dead-ahead view of this spectacular cataract. Lester is a commanding falls in a steep section of the gorge, with a sheer wall at the top where the river splits a wedge into a chute of rapids and explodes with aplomb over the crest to the main 30-foot plunge. The river sails past the rag-

Waterfalls frolic through a narrow gorge. STACY DORN

ged, jagged black rock cliff to a large, deep pool of root beer–colored water and falls again over a couple of smaller plunges downstream. This is another secluded place with nary a soul in sight.

Option: One more treat lies upstream. Lester River Road heads about 1 mile north from the main park to a small turnout on the river side of the road. From here, a gravel path leads to an elevated view of Twin Falls, or you can choose one of the river access trails for a head-on look at the base of the waterfall.

At the river's banks is a relatively easygoing, 10-foot cascade curving around a wedge of rock on the south side of the river with tall pines and hardwood borders.

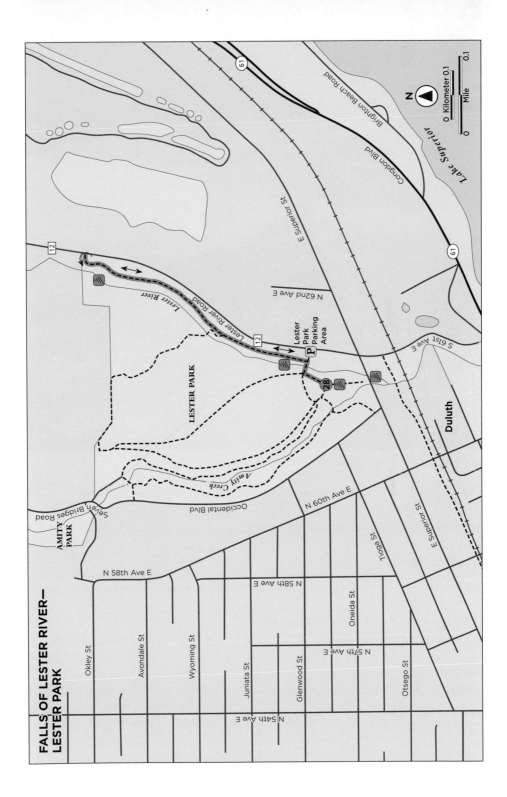

FALLS OF LESTER RIVER—
LESTER PARK

LESTER PARK

AMITY PARK

Seven Bridges Road

Lester River

Lester River Road

Amity Creek

Occidental Blvd

Lester Park Parking Area

Duluth

Lake Superior

Brighton Beach Road

Congdon Blvd

E Superior St

N 62nd Ave E

S 61st Ave E

N 60th Ave E

N 58th Ave E

N 57th Ave E

E Superior St

N 54th Ave E

Okley St

Avondale St

Wyoming St

Juniata St

Glenwood St

Oneida St

Otsego St

Tioga St

N

0 Kilometer 0.1
0   Mile   0.1

A sudsy waterfall on the Lester River. STACY DORN

The waterfall curves off its crest and shoots water in different directions, drops over a big cascade into a pool, and bubbles up into a smaller 2-foot drop below. It is a very pretty falls and, hidden as it is in this gorge, almost always delivers solitude.

Miles and Directions

0.0 From the Superior Street trailhead, follow the path along the river to view the first trio of waterfalls.

0.3 Arrive at final waterfall and turnaround point.

0.6 Arrive back at the trailhead.

Twin Falls

0.0 Twin Falls is best viewed from the ridge above the river on Lester River Road, about 1.4 miles north of Superior Street. Park in the turnout on the river side of the road and follow the trail down to river level, or take in the high view from the roadside.

0.2 Arrive at the river and waterfall.

0.4 Arrive back at the trailhead, if you chose the trail to the river.

The North Shore

E ven a single visit leaves its mark. Seeing the big lake up close is an experience, an indelible memory that remains with you like your own shadow. You will return, for the lake's powerful siren song echoes in the orchestra halls of your heart, and to hear it best is to be at its side.

For anyone hailing from the Northland, Lake Superior is part of our lives. It is stunningly beautiful. It is moody and seductive. It is a maelstrom, peace, challenge, inspiration. It is the *Fitz* and Gordon Lightfoot. Deep and icy cold.

As we are traditionally, instinctively, excitedly inclined to do around here, we get out there to these places to feel and touch and smell and just be, and Superior invites us to her waters and shores to take a deep breath of wild. Lake Superior captivates its audiences, be it an innocent child tossing polished round rocks from a beach or the hardened crew of an immense freighter battling 30-foot swells. Even in its absence, the mighty lake's hypnotic waters remain saturated in our memories, until we return again to her embrace. Superior's North Shore is a conduit to our daydreams: a long and winding journey from Duluth to Grand Portage through magical lands of quiet bays; high, rugged cliffs, deep gorges, scenic rivers—and waterfalls!

Boisterous in the spring, composed and approachable in summer, shy and tranquil in autumn, the waterfalls of "The Shore" invite us to explore, frolic, listen, or simply watch. Water plunges with abandon through pleats in ancient mountains. It explodes in cannon blasts over crests of soaring cliffs and whispers beneath rustic footbridges. The northern shoreline of Superior boasts 150 miles of unforgettable vistas and quaint towns and secret hideaways. It is decorated with eight dazzling state parks, as well, shining like a string of pearls from Gooseberry Falls to the Canadian border, offering some of the very best in liquid North Country scenery. Come along, and let's get to know the Northland's moving landscape.

29 French River Falls

Hidden in plain sight from the highway, this cedar-fringed waterfall is one of the prettiest on the North Shore.

Waterway: French River
Waterfall beauty: 5
Distance: 0.2 mile out and back
Difficulty: Easy
Hiking time: About 10 minutes
Trail surface: Natural
Other trail users: None

Canine compatibility: Leashed pets allowed
Land status: Public
Fees and permits: No fee required
Maps: Regional maps; USGS French River
Trail contacts: North Shore Visitor Guide, PO Box 1342, Grand Marais 55604, northshoreinfo.com

Finding the trailhead: From Duluth, follow the MN 61 Expressway for 6.5 miles north to Ryan Road, just before reaching the French River bridge. Park along Ryan Road. *Note:* Construction was in process at the time of this hike. Conditions and access may be different from what is shown here.
Trailhead GPS: N46 54.057' / W91 54.040'

The Hike

French River Falls is one of the prettiest along this lower section of the North Shore, yet rarely seen by occupants in cars whizzing by on the expressway. A short walk along the ditch below the road leads to a grove of white pine with a head-on, elevated view of the falls, tucked in a gorgeous glen of majestic cedar and conifer. Three sections of the torrent are visible from here, starting with the small cascade way up at the crest. The cascade drops to slide around some boulders on a foamy wave and off a ledge into a large pool. From here the creek blasts through a narrow chute between the rocks to the base and then through a huge drainage tunnel under the highway.

The towering trees make a perfect frame for this postcard setting, and careful steps lead down to the rocks near the creek for closer examination. At creek level, the descent in elevation and the roar of the falls mask the traffic drone above, and with only a slight stretch of imagination, this place feels like it is much farther from civilization.

"Civilization" nearby consists of the tiny community of French River; population: not many. The river itself crashes beneath the highway bridge past the little burg, tantalizingly magnetic in its encouragement to follow.

Quintessential North Country. CASSANDRA BALTES ▶

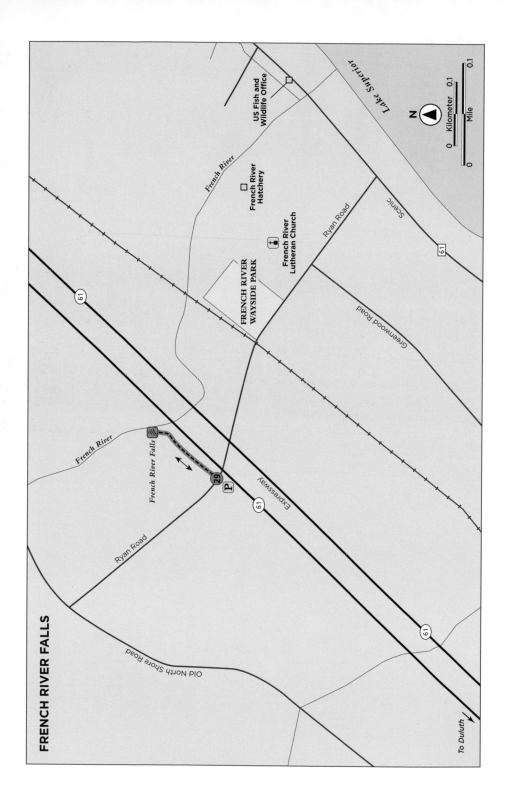

FRENCH RIVER FALLS

French River tumbles through a gorge of vibrant cedars. DAVID TOMLINSON

Miles and Directions

0.0 From Ryan Road, hike north along the roadway path to the river.

0.1 Arrive at the view of the falls.

0.2 Arrive back at Ryan Road.

30 Trestle Bridge Falls

The French River has an encore to its main attraction. Start at the mouth of the river, with shore-side views of Lake Superior, and follow the path upstream for a front-row seat.

Waterway: French River
Waterfall beauty: 3
Distance: 0.7 mile out and back
Difficulty: Easy
Hiking time: About 20 minutes
Trail surface: Paved and natural
Other trail users: None

Canine compatibility: Leashed pets allowed
Land status: Public
Fees and permits: No fee required
Maps: Regional maps; USGS French River
Trail contacts: North Shore Visitor Guide,
PO Box 1342, Grand Marais 55604,
northshoreinfo.com

Finding the trailhead: From Duluth, follow the MN 61 Expressway for 6.5 miles north to Ryan Road. Turn right on Ryan Road and follow it 0.3 mile east to Scenic Highway 61. Turn left, cross the French River bridge and park in the lot on the right, at lakeside.
Trailhead GPS: N46 53.988' / W91 53.537'

The Hike

This is a great little hike before even taking a step. The trailhead happens to be near the mouth of the river, with horizon-stretching views of Lake Superior, and is a great place to skip rocks or watch waves rumble in.

Pass a series of small cascades on the way upstream, and then the fish ladder locations. The Minnesota Department of Natural Resources used to conduct native fish breeding programs here; when they were big and strong, staff turned the fish loose and away they went. It's still amazing to me how fish can climb ladders.

The fern-lined trail is a scenic stroll through balsam and aspen woods. Near the bridge are more cascades stretched out in a frothing dance among the rocks. There are great places hither and yon to sit back and take in the mood of the place.

More cascades and falls materialize a short way upstream, along with a couple of swimming holes for spontaneous dips on hot summer days. As you near the railroad trestle bridge, look for a little three-tier falls that steps down just below the bridge.

The French River below the trestle bridge. CASSANDRA BALTES ▶

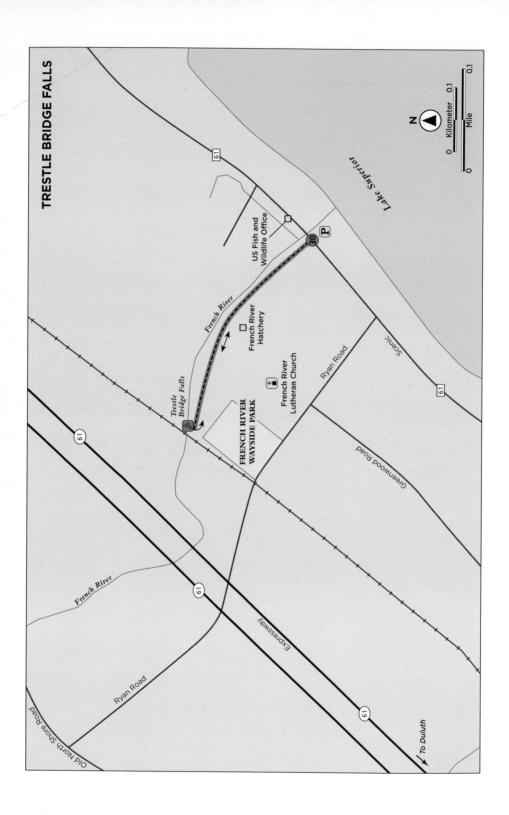

Easygoing cascades on the way to Lake Superior. CASSANDRA BALTES

Miles and Directions

0.0 From the trailhead parking area, cross the highway and head into the woods on the path along the west side of the river.

0.1 Reach the first section of falls. Continue hiking upstream.

0.3 Arrive at the railroad trestle falls.

0.6 Arrive back at the trailhead.

Put Scenic Highway 61 on your North Shore bucket list. From Gitchi Gammi Park to Two Harbors, the original route of this iconic Minnesota roadway is a 20-mile stretch of intimate beaches, quaint villages, and scores of overlooks of the big lake. Cruise easy and soak in the history of the North Shore.

31 Schmidt Creek Falls

Steal away to solitude at this seldom-visited waterfall nestled in a glen of cedar and aspen. It's like hanging out in your very own living postcard.

Waterway: Schmidt Creek
Waterfall beauty: 4
Distance: 0.1 mile out and back
Difficulty: Easy
Hiking time: About 10 minutes
Trail surface: Natural
Other trail users: None

Canine compatibility: Leashed pets allowed
Land status: Public
Fees and permits: No fee required
Maps: Regional maps; USGS French River
Trail contacts: North Shore Visitor Guide, PO Box 1342, Grand Marais 55604, northshoreinfo.com

Finding the trailhead: From Duluth, follow the MN 61 Expressway for 6.5 miles north to Ryan Road. Turn left on Ryan Road and go 0.5 mile to a right turn at Old North Shore Road. Cross the French River and shortly turn right on CR 290. Follow this gravel road for 0.4 mile to a dead end at Schmidt Creek.
Trailhead GPS: N46 54.590' / W91 53.662'

The Hike

This pretty falls is cocooned in a scenic glen of cedar and aspen. A very short trail leads to river level and close to the falls. Schmidt Creek tumbles down stairsteps of huge basalt boulders in a distractingly scenic glen of cedar trees and moss-covered roots and rocks. After a final pair of short drops, the creek glides down a ramp of rock, pools, and then drifts onward to Lake Superior. Leaning back against a beefy white pine, I felt sure I had traveled to a fantasy world of wood elves and hobbits. This is an easy-access, count-on-it solitude place I'll return to often.

Miles and Directions

0.0 From the end of the road, hike to the creek and bridge for good views of the falls.
0.1 Arrive back at the trailhead.

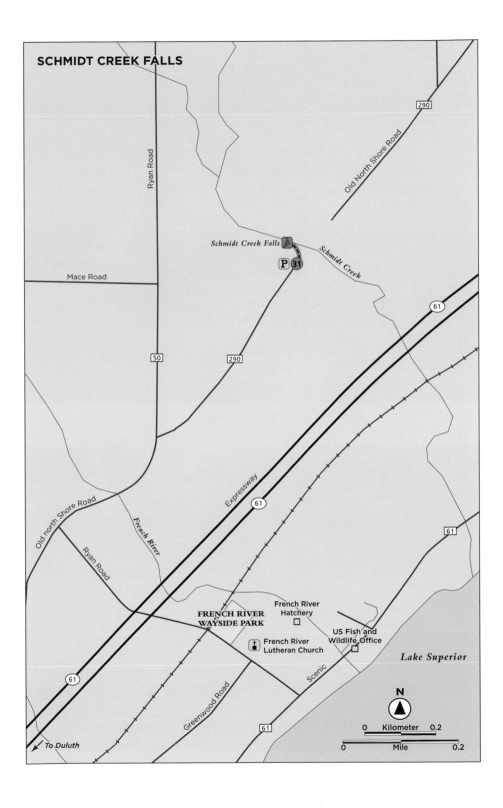

The secluded setting at Schmidt Creek Falls. BRAYDEN MILLS

Late afternoon sun behind the falls. BRAYDEN MILLS

32 First Falls—Knife River

The Knife River is another multiple-waterfall affair. Introducing the show is First Falls, only steps from the wayside and complete with a patio of sloping rock for kicking back and watching the tumbling water.

Waterway: Knife River
Waterfall beauty: 3.5
Distance: 0.2 mile out and back
Difficulty: Easy
Hiking time: About 10 minutes
Trail surface: Natural
Other trail users: None

Canine compatibility: Leashed pets allowed
Land status: Public
Fees and permits: No fee required
Maps: Regional maps; USGS Knife River
Trail contacts: North Shore Visitor Guide, PO Box 1342, Grand Marais 55604, northshoreinfo.com

Finding the trailhead: From Duluth, follow the MN 61 Expressway for 13 miles northeast to the wayside and historical marker just past the river bridge. A trail at the west end of the parking area leads to the river and waterfall.
Trailhead GPS: N46 56.857' / W91 47.537'

The Hike

The watershed of the Knife River is immense, with the West Branch of the Knife and the Little Knife River forming two long wishbone forks that poke far into the heavily forested land west of Two Harbors. As the two forks join and become the Knife River proper, the river's course resembles a child's random scribbles, or a succession of tiny blue, pointy mountains on a map. The erratic route creates a quickly flowing stream with sections of rapids; steep, wooded cliffs; and waterfalls.

It is a short walk from the parking area to First Falls. Follow the path to the huge rock veranda just below the falls. The river splits at the crest of the falls and trips over rock platform steps of varying height. Time your visit right and you'll be treated to very determined steelhead trout fighting their way upstream to mellower spawning sites.

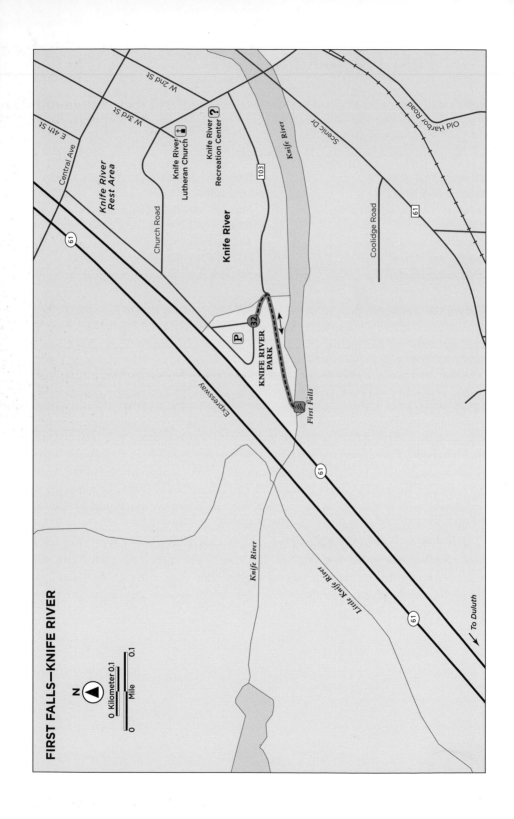

The twin plunges of First Falls. BRAYDEN MILLS

Miles and Directions

0.0 From the trailhead, follow the path to the river and waterfall.

0.1 Retrace your steps to return.

0.2 Arrive back at the trailhead.

The Knife River's bed of sharp rocks gave rise to its Ojibwe-inspired name.

33 Second Falls–Knife River

An invigorating hike on the incomparable Superior Hiking Trail leads through elegant northern forest to this compact but handsome waterfall.

Waterway: Knife River
Waterfall beauty: 4
Distance: 1.2 miles out and back
Difficulty: Easy to moderate
Hiking time: About 1 hour
Trail surface: Natural
Other trail users: None

Canine compatibility: Leashed pets allowed
Land status: Public
Fees and permits: No fee required
Maps: Regional maps; USGS Knife River
Trail contacts: North Shore Visitor Guide, PO Box 1342, Grand Marais 55604, northshoreinfo.com

Finding the trailhead: From Duluth, follow the MN 61 Expressway for 0.4 mile past the Knife River bridge and turn left (north) on Shilhon Road. Follow the road for about 0.7 mile to a dead end and parking area. Look for the trail at the north end of the lot.
Trailhead GPS: N46 57.168' / W91 48.330'

The Hike

Another destination on the Knife River is Second Falls, and a hearty hike takes you there. The trail, a spur of the Superior Hiking Trail, immediately dives into dense stands of huge, old pines and scattered aspen and birch. The river comes into view to the left, at the bottom of a steep, wooded ridge, and the trail follows the river all the way to the falls. It is a wonderful stroll through these old woods, with chickadees greeting the day and squirrels chattering double time from verandas of nearby tree branches. Only a short way in, a spur trail leads to the river and an especially scenic stage of cedar and pine ushering the river over a rock ledge.

After some meandering, the trail reaches a junction that splits either to the waterfall or to Knife River Village, a quaint little community close to the mouth of the town's namesake river. A sign at the junction indicates that Second Falls and the Superior Hiking Trail are just 0.5 mile away. A short way along is the site of an 1899 copper mine, existing today as a deep hole in the ground filled halfway with murky water. It's intriguing and eerily mysterious.

The path continues on bouncy pine needle tread through knee-high fern forests as it nears the falls. Second Falls roars louder than its size, and you hear it long before you see it. A spur trail branches off and drops down a long flight of square, wooden steps to a rock platform right in front of the action. This waterfall tumbles only about 6 feet or so, but the frothy copper water makes its fall with verve into

Second Falls stairsteps over flat-topped boulders. BRAYDEN MILLS ▶

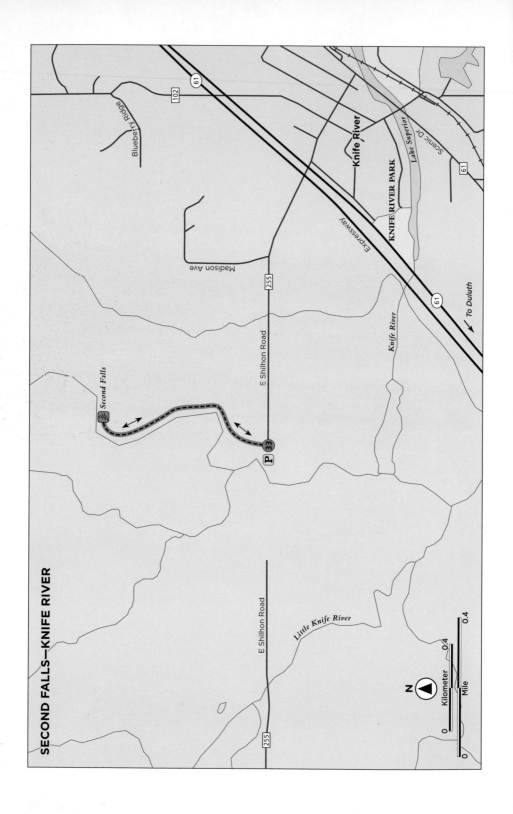

SECOND FALLS—KNIFE RIVER

The Knife River stairsteps through a pine forest. BRAYDEN MILLS

the churning pool below. The river is loaded with dramatic rock formations here, and if the water level cooperates, it's easy to hop out there and scramble around. This is another waterfall big on solitude and perfect for an extended visit. Plan to take a picnic and stay awhile.

Miles and Directions

0.0 From the trailhead, follow the path into the woods. Bear right at the junction with a spur trail.

0.1 Arrive at the river and spur trail to the waterfalls. Continue on the main trail to Second Falls.

0.6 Arrive at Second Falls. Retrace your tracks to return.

1.2 Arrive back at the trailhead.

34 Middle and Lower Falls–Gooseberry Falls State Park

One of Minnesota's most popular state parks, Gooseberry does visitors proud with a four-pack of beauteous waterfalls, which adorn calendars and postcards all over the state. Set aside a full day to explore.

Waterway: Gooseberry River
Waterfall beauty: 5
Distance: 1 mile lollipop loop
Difficulty: Easy
Hiking time: About 30 minutes
Trail surface: Paved and natural
Other trail users: None
Canine compatibility: Leashed pets allowed

Land status: State park
Fees and permits: Fee required
Maps: Gooseberry Falls State Park map; USGS Split Rock Point
Trail contacts: Gooseberry Falls State Park, 3206 Hwy. 61 E., Two Harbors 55616, (218) 595-7100, www.dnr.state.mn.us/state_parks/gooseberry_falls

Finding the trailhead: From Two Harbors, follow MN 61 for about 13 miles north to the park entrance. Various trails start at the visitor center. Follow the Falls Loop Trail for direct access to the waterfalls.
Trailhead GPS: N47 08.460' / W91 28.173'

The Hike

Gooseberry is one of Minnesota's most visited state parks, highlighted by five dramatic waterfalls, camping on Lake Superior's shore, and nearly 20 miles of hiking, biking, and skiing trails. Access to the falls couldn't be easier, by means of the visitor center and Gateway Plaza. The striking visitor center, constructed almost entirely with recycled materials, includes a nature store and trail center packed with information about the park and area history. Keep in mind that the park's popularity, especially the waterfalls, brings in lots of people. Some days visitors are scattered all over the rocks like so many ants at a honeybee picnic, and it can be a challenge just to get an unobstructed look at the falls. Take the time to see Upper Falls too, or take a short hike farther upstream to uncrowded Fifth Falls.

The beautiful Middle and Lower falls live up to their billing as the park's main attraction. The river roars over rugged cliffs of billion-year-old volcanic bedrock in two giant stairsteps. The first tier, Middle Falls, drops in a wide curtain and eddies in small pools around giant lumps of stone. Lower Falls splits at a large island of rock and trees, plunging in two separate cascades to a large pool below. From here it meanders a short distance to Lake Superior. The river ultimately drops 60 feet over these two steps, sometimes in a frothy rage after spring snowmelt or heavy rain, other times in

Sheer veils of Lower Falls. JIM HOFFMAN

just a pleasant shower. Trails lead right to the falls, and when water level obliges it is possible to walk out onto the rocks for an up-close experience not typically available at large waterfalls like this. The Falls Loop Trail follows the river to a footbridge crossing the river and a stellar view of both waterfalls in the gorge upstream. The River View Trail takes off from here and makes a short journey through lowland foliage to Agate Beach and fantastic views of Lake Superior. Look for herring gulls, loons, and bald eagles; spring and fall bring many species of migratory birds along this portion of the North Shore Flyway. Look for unique species of arctic-alpine plants, as well, which thrive in the distinct climate moderated by the immense waters of the big lake.

The main loop continues on a climb to the top of the ridge and shows off Middle Falls from a high overlook. At the highway footbridge, hike back across for the return to the visitor center.

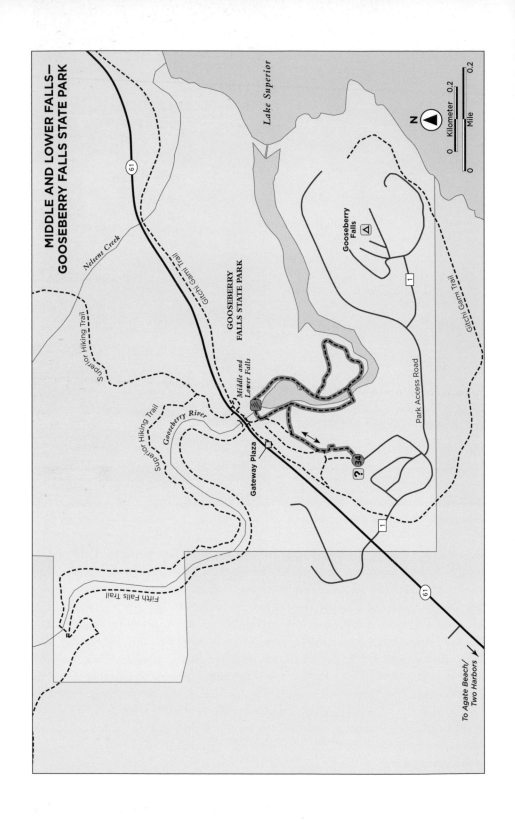

MIDDLE AND LOWER FALLS—
GOOSEBERRY FALLS STATE PARK

Top: A grand display at Middle Falls. BRAYDEN MILLS
Above: Middle Falls in winter. JIM HOFFMAN

Miles and Directions

0.0 From the visitor center, hike the Falls Loop Trail toward the river, bearing right at the first junction.

0.1 Turn right at this next junction, descending a short ridge to Middle Falls (and a view of Lower Falls).

0.3 Arrive at a footbridge across the river. Cross here and return on the east-side trail.

0.6 Junction with footbridge at the highway. Cross back over to the west side.

1.0 Arrive back at the visitor center.

35 Upper and Fifth Falls—Gooseberry Falls State Park

Only a short hike from the hubbub around the main attraction waterfalls, Upper Falls is radiant as a new bride and sparks a fire to explore even deeper into the park to visit Fifth Falls for an unforgettable day in the woods.

Waterway: Gooseberry River
Waterfall beauty: 5
Distance: 0.5 mile out and back for Upper Falls; 2-mile lollipop loop for Fifth Falls
Difficulty: Easy to moderate
Hiking time: About 25 minutes for Upper Falls; 90 minutes for Fifth Falls
Trail surface: Paved and natural
Other trail users: None

Canine compatibility: Leashed pets allowed
Land status: State park
Fees and permits: Fee required
Maps: Gooseberry Falls State Park map; USGS Split Rock Point
Trail contacts: Gooseberry Falls State Park, 3206 Hwy. 61 E., Two Harbors 55616, (218) 595-7100, www.dnr.state.mn.us/state_parks/gooseberry_falls

Finding the trailhead: From Two Harbors, follow MN 61 for about 13 miles north to the park entrance. Various trails start at the visitor center. Start on the path behind the visitor center that heads toward the highway bridge.
Trailhead GPS: N47 08.460' / W91 28.173'

The Hike

Gooseberry is already a beautiful park with the marquee attraction of the big falls and visitor center, but there's more right around the corner. The park made access to its falls and trails very user friendly, with paved pathways leading every which way to explore the sights. Hike past the distinctive masonry of the 300-foot-long Castle in the Park stone wall, built in the 1930s by the Civilian Conservation Corps, and located beneath the highway on the way to Upper Falls. In a made-to-order postcard setting, Upper Falls thunders 30 feet in twin cascades over a shallow crescent of rock ledges nestled in a vibrant grove of tall cedar and pine dappled with birch and aspen. The main overlook offers a superb head-on view. A trail through the cedars, damp with mist from the falls, leads right to the crest where you can feel the water's roar at your feet. Several ancient lava flows can be seen here, the result of an unfathomable split in the earth along the present-day North Shore.

There is something else special here, too. Crowds are noticeably thinner than downstream. As is the case with most any park or similar attraction, the number of people drops dramatically with even small increases in distance or difficulty from a trailhead. That's great news for adventuresome hikers, and some real treasures are out

Calendar-worthy shot of Upper Falls. JIM HOFFMAN

there beyond the all-access areas. While most everyone turns back from Upper Falls, a narrow dirt footpath, Fifth Falls Trail, winds through the woods along the west banks of the river to a bridge crossing. Here the Fifth Falls Trail continues its course, and just across the bridge the epic Superior Hiking Trail (SHT) wanders in from the backcountry. Both trails lead to another bridge at Fifth Falls.

Fifth Falls drapes over a conglomerate of sturdy, flat-edged boulders as the river cuts through the bottom of a shallow gorge in a mixed forest of evergreens, aspen, and birch. The Superior Hiking Trail crosses the bridge high above, and roughshod vertical walls of rock climb from the river. Eons of raging water sculpted small caves in the walls, which are accessible when the river is running tame. Hardy cedar and spruce grow from the steep sides of the gorge, and other dense shrubbery crowds the scene. These falls sometimes welcome visitors to rest at the water's edge, or they can rage over the rocks in foamy torrents, demanding instant respect even from a distance. This is an excellent destination to enjoy some solitude and the company of local wildlife. More than 140 species of birds live in or visit the park, as do 46 species of mammals, like white-tailed deer and black bears. This is also a great rendezvous

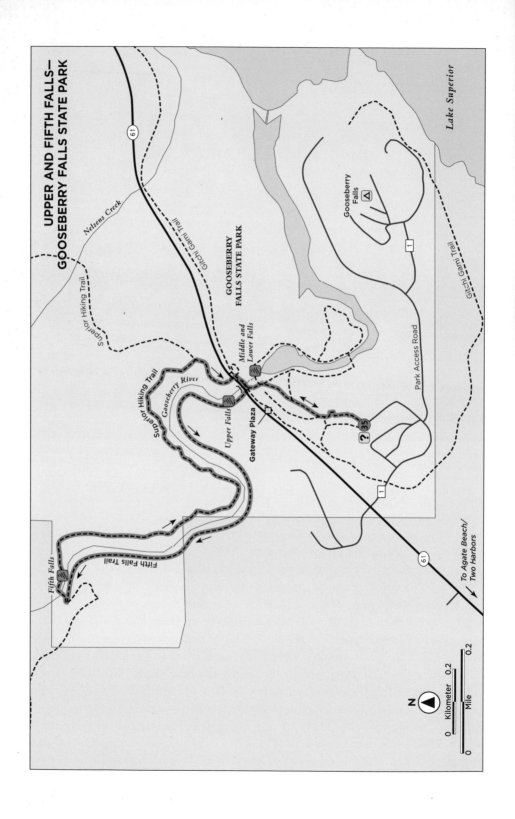

UPPER AND FIFTH FALLS—
GOOSEBERRY FALLS STATE PARK

Lake Superior

Gooseberry
Falls

GOOSEBERRY
FALLS STATE PARK

Middle and
Lower Falls

Upper Falls

Gateway Plaza

Gooseberry River

Superior Hiking Trail

Fifth Falls Trail

Fifth Falls

Superior Hiking Trail

Gitchi Gami Trail

Nelsens Creek

Gitchi Gami Trail

Park Access Road

? 35

1

1

61

61

To Agate Beach/
Two Harbors

N

Kilometer   0.2
0

Mile
0   0.2

Trail bridge above Fifth Falls. JIM HOFFMAN

point or springboard to the SHT and many miles of backcountry trails in the park. Bring a mountain bike in the cool fall months. In the winter the cross-country skiing here is out of this world.

Miles and Directions

0.0 From the visitor center, follow the paved Falls Loop Trail toward the Gateway Plaza and the highway bridge. Cross under the highway and continue to the falls.

0.2 Arrive at the Upper Falls overlook. Spur trails wander through the woods to the crest of the falls. Retrace your steps back, or continue upriver to reach Fifth Falls.

0.9 Arrive at the bridge above Fifth Falls. Enjoy the view, then continue across to the east side of the river and the Superior Hiking Trail. Follow the SHT back downstream.

1.5 Cross another bridge over the river.

2.0 Arrive back at the visitor center.

The masterful stonework, masonry, and all-around outdoor artistry seen at Gooseberry and many state parks along the North Shore is courtesy of the Civilian Conservation Corps (CCC). Born of President Roosevelt's work relief program in 1933, the CCC provided work for millions of Great Depression-era young men and instilled a nationwide awareness of natural resources conservation. Of the many significant accomplishments of this stalwart group, the CCC planted nearly *3 billion* trees in America's reforestation efforts.

36 Nelsens Creek Falls– Gooseberry Falls State Park

Leave the crowds behind and hike a little-traveled chunk of Gooseberry Falls State Park to spend time with this intimate waterfall on Nelsens Creek.

Waterway: Nelsens Creek
Waterfall beauty: 3
Distance: 2-mile lollipop loop
Difficulty: Moderate
Hiking time: About 90 minutes
Trail surface: Paved and natural
Other trail users: None
Canine compatibility: Leashed pets allowed

Land status: State park
Fees and permits: Fee required
Maps: Gooseberry Falls State Park map; USGS Split Rock Point
Trail contacts: Gooseberry Falls State Park, 3206 Hwy. 61 E., Two Harbors 55616, (218) 595-7100, www.dnr.state.mn.us/state_parks/gooseberry_falls

Finding the trailhead: From Two Harbors, follow MN 61 for about 13 miles north to the park entrance. Various trails start at the visitor center. Start on the Gateway Plaza path behind the visitor center that heads toward the highway bridge.
Trailhead GPS: N47 08.460' / W91 28.173'

The Hike

A short jaunt inland from the big lake and into Gooseberry's stately forests treats hikers to a secluded waterfall in a pretty glen of green ferns and mosses and bright white birch. On the Gitchi Gummi Trail, follow the left fork and climb the hill along stone-walled switchbacks. There is a great view of Lake Superior from the top of the hill. Pass the log shelter and the trail turns hard right, paralleling Nelsens Creek. Look for a skinny spur trail on the left and go that way. The path drops steeply to creekside. With an overture of murmuring from a gathering of smaller cascades, the creek aims for a chute through a cleft in a huge heap of dark gray rock and sprays into a quiet pool below, rests a bit, and then tips over a final short drop to another pool. It is a very picturesque setting, flanked by pines and mossy rocks and logs—perfect for settling back against the smooth, wide trunk of an aspen and listening to the creek's serenade. Time your visit to this little-known gem at high water for the best waterfall vibe, and in the fall for the aspens' golden glow.

The trail curves back south and west, with several lookouts to stellar Lake Superior views, including a cover shot view right at the shore. The trail soon closes its loop back at the switchback junction and the last section to the bridge.

Gitchi Gummi Trail with Lake Superior view. BRAYDEN MILLS ▶

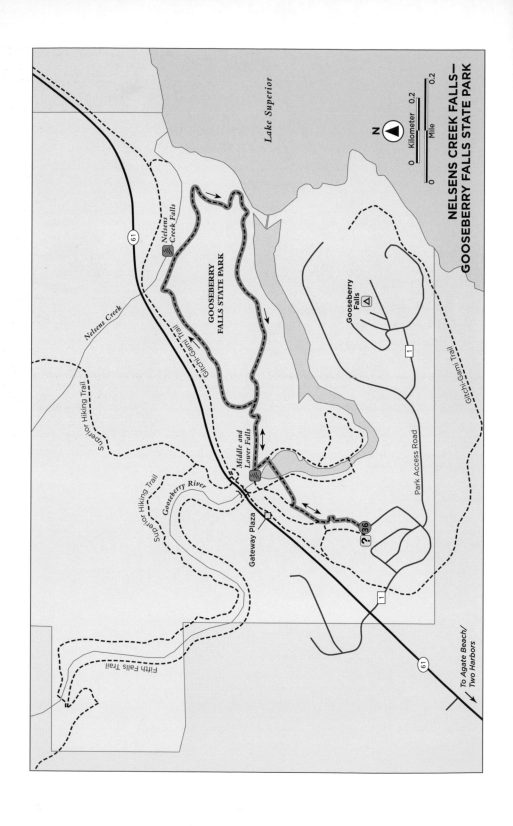

NELSENS CREEK FALLS—
GOOSEBERRY FALLS STATE PARK

Lake Superior

N

0   Kilometer   0.2

0   Mile   0.2

GOOSEBERRY
FALLS STATE PARK

Nelsens Creek Falls

61

Nelsens Creek

Gitchi-Gami Trail

Superior Hiking Trail

Gooseberry River

Superior Hiking Trail

Fifth Falls Trail

Gooseberry Falls

Middle and Lower Falls

Gateway Plaza

? 36

Park Access Road

Gitchi-Gami Trail

1

1

61

To Agate Beach/
Two Harbors

X marks the spot at Nelsens Creek. BRAYDEN MILLS

Miles and Directions

0.0 From the visitor center, follow the paved path past the stone wall and across the river on the MN 61 footbridge. Turn right and then left at the Gitchi Gummi Trail.

0.4 Turn left and climb the switchbacks.

1.0 Arrive at the falls. Continue the loop south and west back to the highway bridge.

2.0 Arrive back at the visitor center.

37 Falls of Split Rock River

This is the waterfall mother lode, with upward of *a dozen* falls rumbling down the lower reaches of the Split Rock River. Get the camera ready and spend the day stocking up on liquid memories.

Waterway: Split Rock River
Waterfall beauty: 4–5
Distance: Roughly 8 miles out and back for all waterfalls
Difficulty: Moderate to difficult
Hiking time: About 6 hours
Trail surface: Natural
Other trail users: None
Canine compatibility: Leashed pets allowed

Land status: State park
Fees and permits: Fee required
Maps: Split Rock Lighthouse State Park map; USGS Split Rock Point
Trail contacts: Split Rock Lighthouse State Park, 3755 Split Rock Lighthouse Rd., Two Harbors 55616, (218) 595-7625, www.dnr.state.mn.us/state_parks/split_rock_lighthouse

Finding the trailhead: From Two Harbors, follow MN 61 for 19 miles northeast to the wayside parking area on the left. The trail starts directly from the back side of the lot.
Trailhead GPS: N47 10.925' / W91 24.569'

The Hike

There are so many waterfalls on the Split Rock River, it is difficult not to spend the whole day wandering up and down in the midst of all this north woods finery. Depending on what time of year you visit this southern section of the state park and how far you are prepared to hike, you'll find around a dozen significant falls on just a few miles of the river. This is a truly special place to see these falls, as they are invisible to casual passersby on the highway, and the hike is long enough that it eliminates nearly all the weekend crowds.

The first section of trail is a spur leading to the Superior Hiking Trail (SHT), passing through gorgeous stands of birch, aspen, maple, and intermittent pine. The path rolls over hills and short footbridges crossing tiny tributary streams, all with a chorus of birdsong overhead. The river is calm and moves at a relaxed pace off to the right.

The forest is blissfully silent all the way to the 0.5-mile junction with the official Superior Hiking Trail. A left turn goes to Gooseberry Falls State Park, but we'll go right here, following the sign for the Split Rock Bridge. A series of wooden steps descends to the first waterfall. You can hear it down behind the trees, and the last step leads to an ethereal glen of vibrant cedar, with a small fire pit in an adjacent alcove. It is shaded here, in dense woods of ferns and mosses and giant trees. A short footbridge

South Ridge Falls plies a shallow gorge. BRAYDEN MILLS ▶

Shadow Glen Falls at Split Rock River. BRAYDEN MILLS

Cedar Lace Falls and its namesake foliage. BRAYDEN MILLS

reveals what hides away in here. Shadow Glen Falls is a magical column of trickling water, with a hypnotic song echoing from a curved rock amphitheater. An audience of attentive boulders and river rocks enjoys the performance, next to a steep cliff wall decorated with a soft fleece of moss. There is a calm pool front and center, and a backstage trail leads close to the falls. This is the West Branch of the Split Rock River, at its tail end just before it meets the main river only a stone's throw from here.

It is difficult to leave, to be sure, but continue up the steep set of stairs on the other side of this little valley and trudge over the ridge, heading toward the river's main channel. The trail flirts with the river's banks just for a moment and then darts back to climb a steep hill. A high, wooded ridge rises on the opposite side of the river, with the sound of a significant waterfall way below. Alas, this one can't be seen through thick summer foliage, so plan on views in spring or fall.

Just over the crown of the ridge, listen for another roar. The river rounds a bend far below and takes a nose-dive down South Ridge Falls, a ruggedly handsome brute that starts with a modest cascade, pools near a pile of horizontally stacked rocks, shoots into a wide fan of rapids, and then takes a hard left to blast through a narrow chute. All of this is visible past the trunks of huge pine, cedar, and birch trees up on

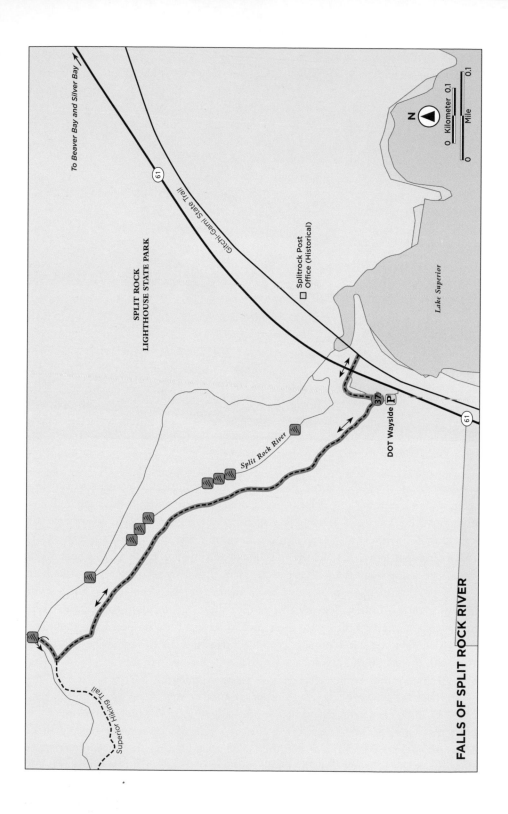

FALLS OF SPLIT ROCK RIVER

the hill. Getting down to river level is dangerous and not recommended, so soak in the balcony view for a while and head upriver to see what else might be waiting.

For starters, here the trail goes along and in a stunning deep gorge, reinforcing our affection for every step on the SHT. The path is impeccably maintained over spider-web roots, hard-packed dirt, small boulders, and footbridges and travels through some of the most exhilarating landscapes on the planet. Make a point to bring a backpack next time and spend a few days roaming.

The trail bends around for a nice view of the crest of South Ridge Falls and drops farther into the gorge. A fifth falls is just around the corner. Split Rock Cascades is a small, two-tiered cascade, each tier about 4 feet tall, at the base of a gorgeous, high-walled red rock canyon. This is a gentle prelude of the next attraction, just ahead where the river parts a thick stand of trees.

Cedar Lace Falls is a dreamy waterfall caressing a slide of brown rocks with a soft shower of lacy white. Nearly ten separate, delicate liquid tendrils sluice over rounded rock ledges to a large, calm pool, flanked to the west by a dense canvas of bulbous cedar trees. The upper section falls 10 feet to a flat ledge and then spreads into a wide slide with another curvy cataract off to the side. It is a heavenly setting sure to capture your attention for a long while. The trail curves up and right past the crest for a great close-up look, too. This is another of those places to settle in and spend some time watching the water dance.

A steep hill leads to yet another falls, this one very difficult to see through the foliage, but you can hear it, and even the obscured view reveals a pretty cascade, shorter and leaner than the others, but giving away nothing in the way of north woods beauty. With only a brief break in the action, you arrive at Two Forks Falls as the gorge opens wider. This is a gorgeous waterfall, beginning at a huge, flat table of rock and falling into two main chutes of white; one sliding down a gently angled slab of rock, and the other falling from a horseshoe-shaped hollow in an adjacent rock pile. There is another hump of boulders at the base, a pool of foam, and a smaller cascade below. Brilliant green cedars again adorn the ridges above the river.

A short hike upstream leads to the finale waterfall. A pair of narrow chutes funnels the river in a 20-foot flurry past a rock outcrop, with bright orange peel–colored lichen on the adjacent cliff walls.

Bonus points are awarded on this trail for being able to see the waterfalls twice on this out-and-back hike. That's like seeing at least *eighteen* waterfalls in one day!

Miles and Directions

0.0 Set out from the highway trailhead, hiking northwest on the SHT spur trail.

0.5 Go right (straight ahead) at the SHT's Gooseberry Falls junction.

1.2 Arrive at the next trio of waterfalls.

2.8 Pass Cedar Lace and several more falls.

4.0 Arrive at the final waterfall. Retrace your tracks to the trailhead.

8.0 Arrive back at the highway trailhead.

38 Split Rock Creek Falls– Split Rock Lighthouse State Park

This little waterfall appeared as an unexpected treat on a hike to Day Hill, and is in such a tranquil and picture-perfect setting that it quickly became one of my North Shore favorites.

Waterway: Split Rock Creek
Waterfall beauty: 4
Distance: 3-mile loop with tails
Difficulty: Easy, with one short, difficult climb to the top of Day Hill
Hiking time: About 1 hour
Trail surface: Paved and natural
Other trail users: None
Canine compatibility: Leashed pets allowed

Land status: State park
Fees and permits: Fee required
Maps: Split Rock Lighthouse State Park map; USGS Split Rock Point
Trail contacts: Split Rock Lighthouse State Park, 3755 Split Rock Lighthouse Rd., Two Harbors 55616, (218) 595-7625, www.dnr.state.mn.us/state_parks/split_rock_lighthouse

Finding the trailhead: From Two Harbors, head northeast on MN 61 for 20 miles to the park entrance. Follow the park road to the picnic area and campsite access parking. Start hiking the paved trail along the lake and look for the Day Hill Trail signs.
Trailhead GPS: N47 11.737' / W91 22.778'

The Hike

A single, ferocious storm on Lake Superior in 1905 sent six ships into its cold depths within 12 miles of the Split Rock River. Four years later the Split Rock Light Station was constructed to warn ships away from a similar demise along the North Shore's rocky perils. Keepers at the station shined the Split Rock light for fifty-nine years over the western waters of the lake, and the state of Minnesota acquired the property as a historic site in 1971. Today the restored lighthouse offers tours of the light tower, signal building, and keeper's house. The surrounding state park grounds are equally stunning, with several scenic waterfalls hidden away off the beaten path.

The hiking trails at the shoreline, just a sampling of the more than 14 miles of trails in the park, follow a squiggly path along pebbly beaches and protruding peninsulas. There are several overlooks and otherwise outstanding views of the big lake, and a collection of cart-in campsites are nestled in secluded alcoves of rocks and trees. The first section of the Day Hill Trail travels through here, passing a junction leading to the top of Day Hill. This is a can't-miss side trip on the way to the waterfall. The climb is long but gradual to the base of the summit, and then scrambles steeper over a final ascent of boulders. At the top is one of the most fantabulous views of Lake

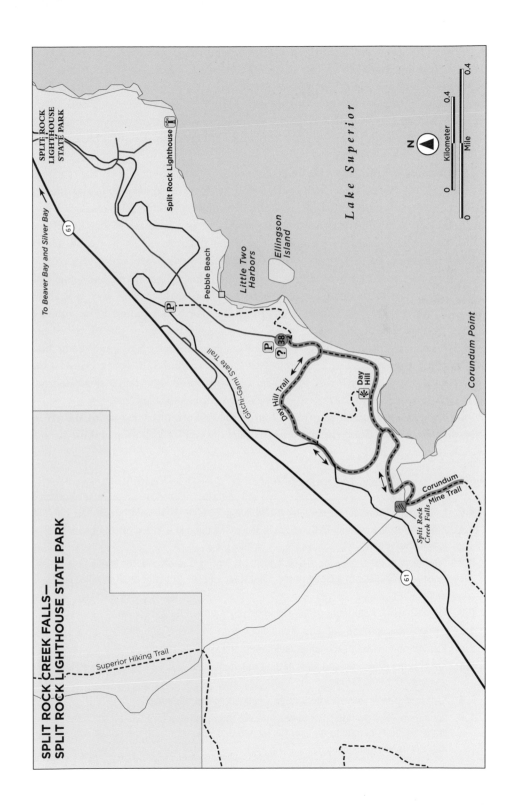

SPLIT ROCK CREEK FALLS—
SPLIT ROCK LIGHTHOUSE STATE PARK

To Beaver Bay and Silver Bay

SPLIT ROCK
LIGHTHOUSE
STATE PARK

61

Split Rock Lighthouse

Pebble Beach

Gitchi-Gami State Trail

P

P

? 38

Day Hill Trail

Day Hill

Little Two Harbors

Ellingson Island

Lake Superior

Corundum
Mine Trail

Split Rock
Creek Falls

61

Corundum Point

Superior Hiking Trail

N

0   0.4
Kilometer
0   0.4
Mile

Superior. The lake unfolds horizon to horizon in all its grandeur, and on a clear day the Apostle Islands are visible nearly 50 miles away toward the south shore. The large, stone fireplace structure perched on the top of this rock is said to have been built around 1900. The fireplace was the first ingredient of a home that Frank Day, a Duluth businessman, intended on building for his sweetheart. Alas, legend has it that the fair maiden did not feel the same way, and left Frank alone with a broken heart and a finely crafted fireplace.

Continuing on the Day Hill Trail takes you to Split Rock Creek Falls, a small waterfall light on drama but well worth a visit, with extraordinary scenery, stunning views of Lake Superior, and access to miles of additional hiking. The creek is a perfect rendition of a babbling brook, murmuring beneath a wooden bridge and down a narrow gap in a shallow rock gorge. The waterfall drops easily over a jumble of square-faced rocks and ledges at various angles, funneling the creek through a narrow chute into a small plunge pool. Dense woods and other foliage adorn the scene, and this quiet section of the trail is tailor made for slowing down and taking it all in. Across the bridge and just a short hike toward the lake is Corundum Point, offering an elevated vantage of jaw-agape views of the rugged beauty of the North Shore. Feel like exploring more of this great park? Roughly another 1.5 miles of scenic hiking on the Corundum Mine Trail leads past Crazy Bay and Split Rock Point to the mouth of the Split Rock River, which sports many more waterfalls a short distance upstream. (See Hike 37, Falls of Split Rock River, for details.)

To return from Corundum Point, follow the mine trail back toward the creek, then follow the path along the shore to the start of the Day Hill loop and the homestretch to the trailhead.

Miles and Directions

0.0 From the trailhead, follow the paved path along the shore to the start of the Day Hill Trail.

0.4 Turn right on the Day Hill Trail, gradually ascending through a mixed forest of spruce, fir, aspen, and maple.

0.7 Junction with the trail to the Day Hill overlook. Turn right and climb the moderately steep grade to breathless (maybe from the hike) views of Lake Superior in all its wild-blue-yonder glory.

0.9 Top of Day Hill. Return the same way when you're done ogling the view.

1.1 Overlook junction; turn left and hike along the paved Gitchi-Gami Trail.

1.2 Turn left on the trail descending back toward the lake.

1.5 Arrive at the lakeshore and start of the Corundum Mine Trail. Turn right. The waterfall is less than 0.1 mile farther.

1.6 Split Rock Creek Falls and footbridge. Continue across the bridge.

1.8 Corundum Point overlook. For bonus miles to the Split Rock River, follow the mine trail to the south. To complete the Day Hill loop, retrace your tracks to the bridge and junction with the uphill spur trail.

2.1 Junction with spur trail; continue straight ahead.

2.4 Junction with start of Day Hill loop. Turn right and follow the path back to the trailhead.

3.0 Arrive back at the trailhead.

The sheer-walled cliff that gives Split Rock Lighthouse its grand view is more than 1 billion years old, heaved up here by a savage uprising of superheated, super-agitated magma. The stalwart and handsome lighthouse, rugged rock cliffs, and curling blue-green waves below are a wilderness masterpiece.

39 Beaver River Falls

Head for Beaver Bay for easy-access waterfalling just steps from your car. The Beaver River plunges through town like the Budweiser Clydesdales, and hides another beauteous waterfall in a secluded getaway upstream.

Waterway: Beaver River
Waterfall beauty: 5
Distance: 0.5 mile out and back to the middle falls, or a handful of steps to the bridge viewpoint
Difficulty: Easy to moderate
Hiking time: About 40 minutes
Trail surface: Paved and natural
Other trail users: None

Canine compatibility: Leashed pets allowed
Land status: Public
Fees and permits: No fee required
Maps: City and regional maps;
USGS Silver Bay
Trail contacts: North Shore Visitor Guide,
PO Box 1342, Grand Marais 55604,
northshoreinfo.com

Finding the trailhead: The falls are visible from the MN 61 bridge in Beaver Bay. Park at the Beaver Bay Wayside at the Lax Lake Road and MN 61 intersection, or along the highway shoulder. A trail also leads from the Lax Lake Road parking area down to the river.
Trailhead GPS: N47 15.598' / W91 17.812'

The Hike

As with most of the streams flowing to Lake Superior from the Laurentian Range, the Beaver River finishes its run with a flurry of activity, cascading steeply over metamorphic rock formations before emptying into the big lake. Beaver River Falls is one of the most easily accessed waterfalls on the North Shore. Its location just below the MN 61 bridge allows a nice look just by slowing down and looking out the car window, but get out and walk closer for a more enjoyable introduction. Standing on the bridge, you are treated to a fantastic view of the first two cascades and a glimpse of the upper falls hidden around the distant bend. Turning downstream, there is an equally spectacular look at Lake Superior and the mouth of the river joining Beaver Bay.

Head along the trail past the woods for a closer look. This long waterfall plunges in three distinct drops separated by short stretches of rapids, with the whole shebang running fast and violent during high water. The lower cascade splits into two separate chutes, one of which hurtles itself down the rocks in a thick mass of white water and rooster tails, while the other spreads thinly over a broad rock face. A huge slab of black gray rock splits the two, and the branches rejoin in a jumble of boulders at their base. A short hike along the trail upstream leads to the middle falls, which thunders over the mammoth rock tables in high water. In less active times of the year, the river

Another North Shore postcard view. JIM HOFFMAN ▶

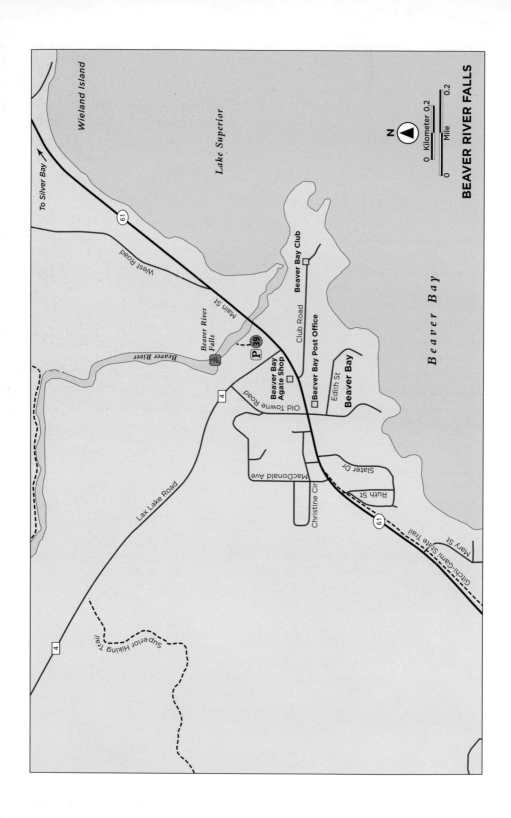

BEAVER RIVER FALLS

A rocky corridor ushers the Beaver River toward Lake Superior. BRAYDEN MILLS

squeezes through a deep splinter right in the middle of the rock, crashing through at scary fast speed and exploding from the base in a wide V of frothy fury. All told, the middle and lower falls each tumble at least 20 feet before riffling off downstream.

One small hump in the trail and a curve left leads to the middle falls. This one is about half the size of its siblings, but striking all the same. The river's copper color clashes with smooth slabs of rock, creating moving dollops of foam sliding on a curvy path to rest briefly in a calm pool and then whisk off along gentle rapids. At the base of the falls are seven huge, rectangular slabs of stone. Some have polished edges; others are pocked with smooth potholes. A couple of them lend visage of an ancient sarcophagus. Above is a large island of trees and boulders stretching to the far side of this cascade. If the water is low, the river may grant access to the island by revealing a stepping-stone trail.

Wander back toward the parking area through glens of aromatic cedar, with carpets of moss and bulbous boulders grizzled with splotches of faded green lichen.

A chute of the Beaver River navigates a boulder field. JIM HOFFMAN

Miles and Directions

0.0 Walk from the parking area to a fine view of the falls from the highway bridge. Want to get closer? From the far eastern end of the parking area, take the dirt trail descending rapidly toward the river.

0.1 Junction with a spur trail to the lower waterfall. Take a look and continue upstream.

0.2 Arrive at trails leading to various vantage points of the two big main falls. Hike around and explore. Return the same way.

0.5 Arrive back at the parking area.

40 Upper Beaver Falls

The Beaver River serves a heaping helping of North Country solitude and elegant forestry on this just-long-enough hike to a lively waterfall.

Waterway: Beaver River
Waterfall beauty: 5
Distance: 2 miles out and back
Difficulty: Moderate
Hiking time: About 1 hour
Trail surface: Natural
Other trail users: None
Canine compatibility: Leashed pets allowed

Land status: Public
Fees and permits: No fee required
Maps: City and regional maps;
USGS Silver Bay
Trail contacts: North Shore Visitor Guide,
PO Box 1342, Grand Marais 55604,
northshoreinfo.com

Finding the trailhead: From Beaver Bay, turn on Lax Lake Road (CR 4) and head north about 0.8 mile to a parking area for the Superior Hiking Trail. Start on the gravel road.
Trailhead GPS: N47 15.967' / W91 18.556'

The Hike

Upper Beaver Falls is another hidden beauty among already opulent North Shore baubles. Even better, this waterfall is far enough removed from the tourist stream that it almost guarantees solitude. Hiking in, the gravel entrance road curves toward the Beaver River and meets a footbridge over the river to a junction with the Superior Hiking Trail (SHT). Go right and parallel the river through an elegant forest of maple, birch, and aspen with an emerald-green fern base layer. The sometimes-rocky trail undulates above the river to an SHT backcountry campsite and the crest of the falls. The river traces a frothy S curve through a jumble of basalt rock piles and stands of towering pine and spruce. This is a linger-worthy slice of the north and well worth a look.

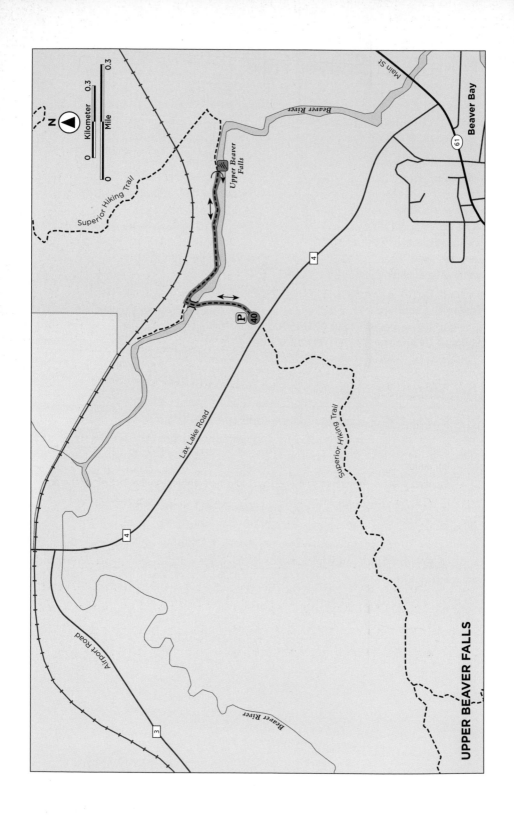

UPPER BEAVER FALLS

The Beaver River churns past aged rock walls. BRAYDEN MILLS

Miles and Directions

0.0 From the trailhead, hike the gravel road along the edge of the woods, past a trio of holding ponds.

0.3 Junction with the footbridge over the river. Cross here and follow the SHT along the river.

1.0 Arrive at the falls. Stay awhile to admire, then retrace your tracks for the return.

2.0 Arrive back at the trailhead parking area.

Beaver Bay is the oldest settlement on Lake Superior's North Shore, established in 1856, just two years prior to Minnesota becoming a state. A group of determined German immigrant brothers from Ohio and their families arrived here by steamer, set down roots, and soon started a lumber mill around a blooming village. Beaver Bay is also the birthplace of John Beargrease, namesake of the long-running sled dog race from Duluth to Grand Portage.

41 Glen Avon Falls

The Beaver River sports yet another lively section of water in close proximity to the pair we visited downstream. Glen Avon Falls conceals itself from most passersby, but introduce yourself and this place will sparkle in your memory long after.

Waterway: Beaver River
Waterfall beauty: 4
Distance: 0.2 mile out and back
Difficulty: Easy
Hiking time: About 10 minutes
Trail surface: Natural
Other trail users: None

Canine compatibility: Leashed pets allowed
Land status: Public
Fees and permits: No fee required
Maps: Regional maps; USGS Silver Bay
Trail contacts: North Shore Visitor Guide, PO Box 1342, Grand Marais 55604, northshoreinfo.com

Finding the trailhead: From Beaver Bay, turn north on Lax Lake Road (CR 4), heading north for 1.6 miles to CR 3. Turn left and follow CR 3 for 1.2 miles to a skinny dirt road on the left. Pull in on this dead-end road and park within sight of the river.
Trailhead GPS: N47 15.955' / W91 20.678'

The Hike

For too many years I sailed along MN 61, anxious to get where I was going. The high-speed journey meant passing right by some of the North Shore's hidden treasures. Glen Avon Falls is one of them. Travel over the ridge from Beaver Bay and you'll see what I mean.

From the quiet county highway, a nearly invisible "road" dribbles into the woods. Walk down the rutted, red-dirt path toward the Beaver River. The river flows from its headwaters in the Superior National Forest through remote woodlands and into this broad valley, flanked to the south and east by a high ridge of dark green forest. Here at the base of the ridge, the river's placid waters emerge from a shaded screen of pine and pick up speed with the onset of an impending drop in elevation. The upper reaches of this waterfall are a torrent of white, plunging 10 feet into a foamy boulder field. From here, the river begins a descent over a long slide of wide rock platforms and shelves, boulders big and small, and hidden eddy pools surrounded by cattails. Little waterfalls frolic here and there, staging their own dramas, and aged cedar trees cling to the tops of immense stone pedestals. The riverside path leads to a view of the middle of the slide where the river tips over another 10-foot drop and then hits a roadblock—a wide rock bench resting smack in the center of the river. For a few moments, the rushing water stops in its tracks, but shortly feels its way along the protruding rock and turns hard right into a narrow alley, bursting through in a wide fan.

A log bridge overlooks Glen Avon Falls. BRAYDEN MILLS

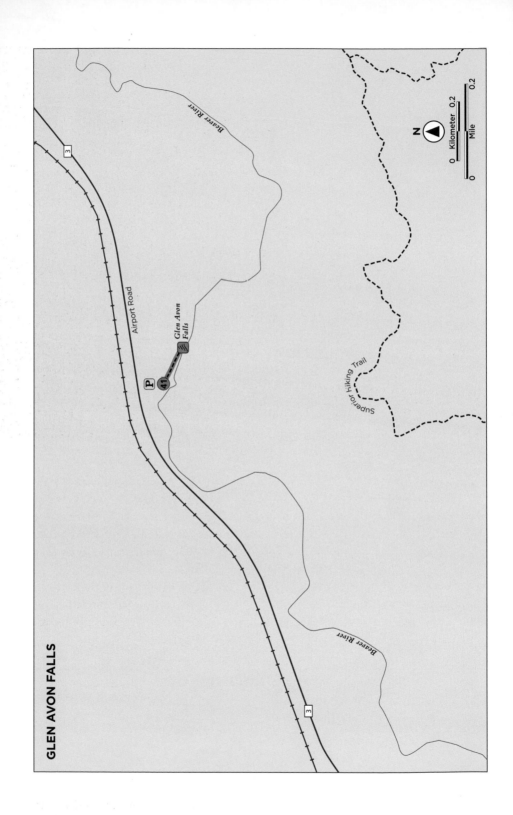

GLEN AVON FALLS

Sublime north woods beauty at Glen Avon Falls. BRAYDEN MILLS

The view downstream from here is fantabulous, as the river bends out of sight into a fold in a canvas of trees. The abundance of rocks create sturdy pathways that lead right into the midst of the falls. Stand on the tip of a tall spire and take in the entire cascade as it rushes around you. Recline on the flat top of a squashed boulder and feel the cold spray of the river. Lean against a tree's trunk and muse about how great it is to be right here in this spot.

Glen Avon's moods change with the seasons. It's fun to come in spring to get to know the falls when they're cranky and splashing water all over the place, or later when a more peaceful scene unfolds and you can sidle up to the river and share secrets.

Miles and Directions

0.0   From the parking area, simply hike the short distance to the river and explore.

0.1   Arrive at river and falls.

0.2   Arrive back at the parking area.

42 High Falls and Two Step Falls— Tettegouche State Park

An author go-to favorite, Tettegouche State Park is like one giant postcard, with nature's finest dressed to the nines on every overlook and shoreline and remote backcountry trail. Plan to stay awhile at this North Shore jewel.

Waterway: Baptism River
Waterfall beauty: 4-5
Distance: 1.4 miles out and back to High Falls; 1.8 miles out and back to Two Step Falls
Difficulty: Difficult
Hiking time: About 90 minutes
Trail surface: Natural
Other trail users: None

Canine compatibility: Leashed pets allowed
Land status: State park
Fees and permits: Fee required
Maps: Tettegouche State Park map; USGS Illgen City
Trail contacts: Tettegouche State Park, 5702 Hwy. 61, Silver Bay 55614, (218) 226-6365, www.dnr.state.mn.us/state_parks/tettegouche

Finding the trailhead: The state park is located 4.5 miles northeast of Silver Bay on MN 61. From the visitor center, follow the campground road to the trailhead parking area. Start hiking at the High Falls Trail sign. This trail leads to both High Falls and Two Step Falls.
Trailhead GPS: N47 20.690' / W91 12.853'

The Hike

Tettegouche State Park bursts at the seams with rugged north woods attractions—postcard memories like Shovel Point; a long, winding stretch of the Superior Hiking Trail; several large, secluded lakes, and four spectacular waterfalls along the scenic Baptism River. The Baptism winds its way from the Sawtooth Mountains through a rugged land of rocks and woods en route to Lake Superior, concluding its passage with verve as it crashes through deep gorges and high walls of woods and rock. Tettegouche is the largest North Shore state park, offering visitors a chance to explore the magical shoreline of Superior, clear, quiet inland lakes, and the rugged beauty of rolling, wooded hills. The majestic virgin pine forests are gone, logged clean in the late 1800s, but the park today is packed full of enchanting northern hardwood forests of aspen and birch, cedar and sugar maple, and scattered stands of Norway and white pine on higher ridges. Twenty-three miles of hiking trails wander through the park, and on foot is the best way to get up-close to the soul of this magical place. Stroll on a self-guided interpretive trail to the scraggly cliffs of Shovel Point, with beauteous views of Lake Superior. Head inland for overnight backpacking trips to remote campsites near Round Mountain or Bear Lake along the mystical Superior Hiking Trail. Day hike to the floating bog on Tettegouche Lake or to the stop-in-your-tracks overlook of Palisade Valley.

High Falls rainbow. JIM HOFFMAN

Whatever your pleasure while hiking through this magnificent park, think back about 1 billion years to get a feel of the basaltic lava flows tilting upward from far beneath Lake Superior (long before there was water there) to form dramatic creations like Shovel Point and the Sawtooth Range. The river gorge itself twists and turns through dense forest and narrows into high ridges and sheer cliffs near the lake. This is where you will find High Falls, the aptly named highest waterfall wholly within Minnesota. An impeccably maintained hiking trail wanders through enchanting forest to a long boardwalk stairway leading down the ridge right to the top of the falls. (The path on the opposite side of the river reaches the falls, too, from the park office and MN 61.) A large platform provides a great view of the gorge downstream and a partial look at the thundering falls. But the best view is on other side.

Follow the trail to a skinny suspension bridge secured to the earth with giant cables, and cross over the river almost directly above the crest of the falls. On the opposite bank the trail curves to a splendid look at High Falls plunging over the crest. The path continues through the woods and down another series of masterfully crafted stairways to a junction heading to river level. Getting down there means negotiating an impressive (read: steep and long) set of stairs. Once there, however, you are rewarded with a head-on look at the gorgeous falls plummeting 70 feet into a wide pool. As a nice bonus, there are rarely other people here, and it feels truly wild. The river continues along the scenic gorge toward another lovely waterfall. Let's go take a look.

Two Step Falls

The other side of the trail fork at the crest of High Falls leads to Two Step Falls, again at the bottom of lots of stairs. Hiking to both of these falls is easily done in one day, with plenty of ogling time to boot. Two Step is a lively number that, true to its name, takes one big step from an upper ledge of rock, churns and froths past tiers of boulders, and enthusiastically drops again in a chute of rapids before settling into a respectable current toward the lake. A handy table of rock right next to the falls allows a chance to sit shoulder to shoulder with the surging stream, especially when the river runs lower.

The park's beauty makes it easy to appreciate the efforts of past groups who saved this place for us to enjoy today. A group of businessmen from Duluth, dubbed the "Tettegouche Club," bought this land from a logging company in 1910 for a retreat

Two Steps Falls glows on a clear day. JIM HOFFMAN

HIGH FALLS AND TWO STEP FALLS—
TETTEGOUCHE STATE PARK

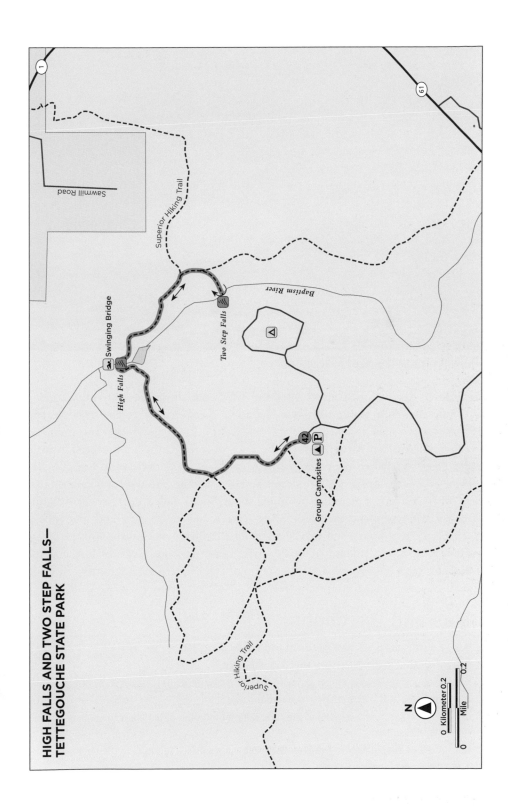

The lower step at Two Steps Falls. BRAYDEN MILLS

and fishing destination. Their stewardship efforts for the area's preservation, along with assistance from groups like The Nature Conservancy, led to the establishment of this area as a state park.

The pine marten darting behind the big spruce is glad to be here, too. And so is the noisy pileated woodpecker hiding in the trees on Shovel Point. Tettegouche's variety of habitat supports a wonderful array of wildlife like these, including more than forty species of mammals roaming about. White-tailed deer are all over the place, as are beavers and snowshoe hares. A keen and lucky eye could spot moose, black bears, river otters, and maybe an elusive timber wolf. Nearly 150 species of birds have also been identified in the park. Look for your favorites in the dense woods and bogs inland, and along the shores of Lake Superior, a migratory route and annual stopover point for several species.

Miles and Directions

0.0 From the trailhead, hike northwest into woods of birch, pine, and aspen.

0.1 Junction with the Superior Hiking Trail; turn right.

0.5 Arrive at suspension bridge above High Falls. Cross the bridge, hike about 500 yards, and turn right at the long stairway down to the river.

0.6 Arrive at the river level view of the falls. Return to the top of the stairs to continue to Two Step Falls.

0.9 Arrive at the stairway to Two Step Falls. Retrace your track to return to the trailhead.

1.8 Arrive back at the trailhead.

43 Cascade Falls—Tettegouche State Park

A robust hike along the Baptism River leads to this crowd-free and elegant waterfall, with perfectly placed boulders for lounging.

Waterway: Baptism River
Waterfall beauty: 4
Distance: 1.6 miles out and back
Difficulty: Moderate
Hiking time: About 1 hour
Trail surface: Natural
Other trail users: None
Canine compatibility: Leashed pets allowed

Land status: State park
Fees and permits: Fee required
Maps: Tettegouche State Park map; USGS Illgen City
Trail contacts: Tettegouche State Park, 5702 Hwy. 61, Silver Bay 55614, (218) 226-6365, www.dnr.state.mn.us/state_parks/tettegouche

Finding the trailhead: The state park is located 4.5 miles northeast of Silver Bay on MN 61. From the visitor center, follow the park road across the river to the campground parking area. The trail starts across the road, following the river upstream.
Trailhead GPS: N47 20.228' / W91 12.144'

The Hike

Cascade Falls are closest to the highway, but only one little-used path goes that way, and crowds of visitors are typically kept at bay by the dramatic scenes just a short stroll from the park entrance, and the dramatic High Falls upstream. Views from the park road bridge are stupendous, overlooking a dreamy setting of a deep gorge of variegated cliffs with broods of pine and aspen and cedar staking claim in solid rock. The river churns far below in a last couple of bends to Lake Superior's expanse. Trails lead to an observation deck looking at a funnel of rapids and down to the mouth of the river at the shore of the lake. It's a beautiful sight, indeed, and a great place to idle away a long summer day just steps inside the park entrance.

The path to the falls sneaks into the woods in the shadow of the Highway 61 bridge, hugging the riverbank through elegant stands of hardwood forest on rolling terrain up and over and around hillocks of rock and assorted shrubbery. Past a half-moon bend in the river, the stately waterfall appears in a shallow cirque of squat cliffs and ragged heaps of boulders. Mixed stands of aspen, birch, and pine garnish the top of a small ridge above the falls. This waterfall looks like an upside-down letter Y, as the river drops into a main stem and then blasts off in one arm of speedy rapids, with the other sliding down the rocks in a wide veil. A deep pool unfurls below, providing a great fishing hole. There are lots of places on the rocks near and in the river to sit and enjoy the venue, and the falls make a comforting tune at just the right volume.

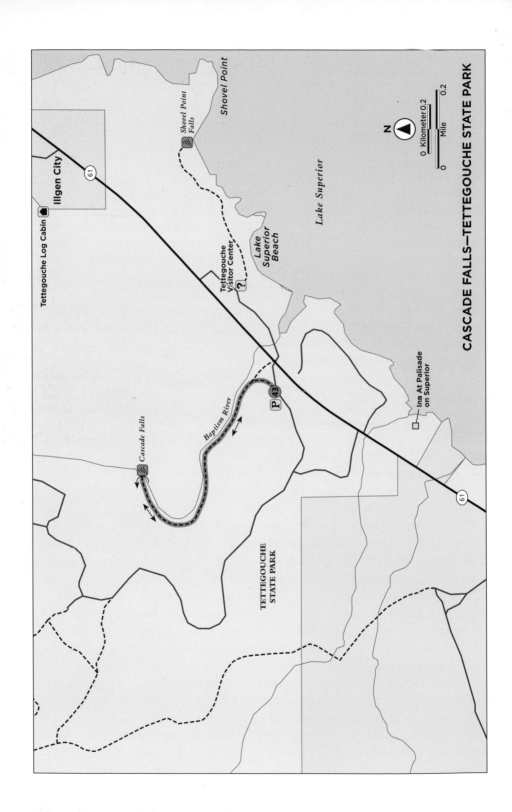

CASCADE FALLS—TETTEGOUCHE STATE PARK

Secluded and scenic Cascade Falls. BRAYDEN MILLS

Miles and Directions

0.0 From the trailhead, hike across the bridge and look for the sign for the Cascades. Head into the woods and hike along the river.

0.8 Arrive at the waterfall. About face to return.

1.6 Arrive back at the trailhead.

44 Shovel Point Falls– Tettegouche State Park

Shovel Point is a legendary chunk of North Shore rock and an all-time author favorite for great hiking and powerful inspiration. Along the trail, an under-the-radar waterfall slides through a skinny gorge on final approach to Lake Superior. Don't miss the wooden bench at creekside for a cozy interlude.

Waterway: Unnamed creek
Waterfall beauty: 3.5
Distance: 0.5 mile out and back
Difficulty: Easy
Hiking time: About 20 minutes
Trail surface: Natural
Other trail users: None
Canine compatibility: Leashed pets allowed

Land status: State park
Fees and permits: Fee required
Maps: Tettegouche State Park map;
USGS Illgen City
Trail contacts: Tettegouche State Park, 5702 Hwy. 61, Silver Bay 55614, (218) 226-6365, www.dnr.state.mn.us/state_parks/tettegouche

Finding the trailhead: The state park is located 4.5 miles northeast of Silver Bay on MN 61. Start from the visitor center parking area on the paved trail.
Trailhead GPS: N47 20.330' / W91 11.667'
Note: This little waterfall ebbs and flows with levels of rainfall or snowmelt.

The Hike

This is a slender little waterfall, largely dependent on ample water flow to even flow at all, but the setting is sublime. No trip to Tettegouche is complete without a hike to Shovel Point, and this waterfall is right on the way.

Tettegouche is one of my favorite go-to destinations, and this short hike is one continuous highlight reel of stop-in-your-tracks scenery. The trail hugs close to the edge of a cliff high above Lake Superior, curving through a handsome forest of maple, pine, birch, and aspen. A cleft in the ridge contains the skinny creek, at the base of a long set of steps. The creek tumbles over the edge here and drops about 30 feet to Lake Superior. Aside from being on the water in a vessel of some kind, it is rare on an inland hike to see the confluence of a waterfall with the lake, and that in itself is a treat. A spur trail leads down to a cozy bench for a sweet view of the waterfall.

Soak it in, and be sure to continue to Shovel Point and one of the most treasured and stunning views to be had of Lake Superior and its powerfully beautiful shoreline.

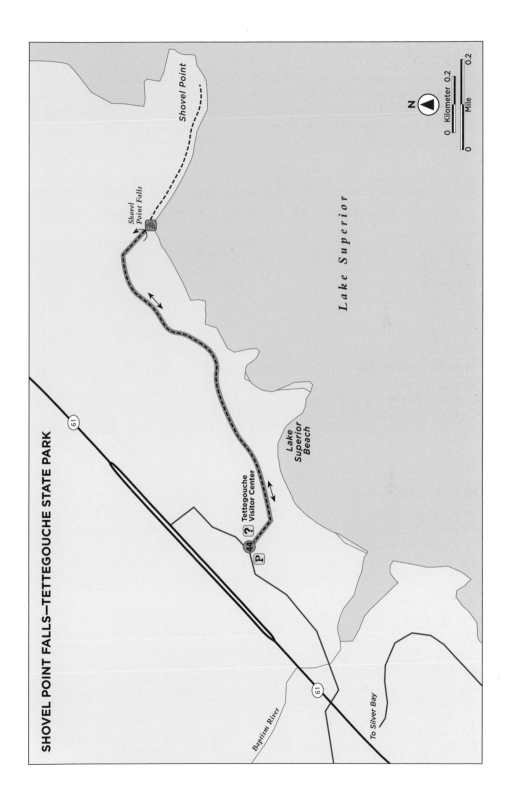

SHOVEL POINT FALLS—TETTEGOUCHE STATE PARK

Shovel Point

Shovel Point Falls

Tettegouche Visitor Center

?

44

P

Lake Superior Beach

L a k e   S u p e r i o r

61

61

Baptism River

To Silver Bay

N

0 Kilometer 0.2

0 Mile 0.2

Miles and Directions

0.0 From the parking area, hike the Shovel Point Trail along the high ridge above the lake. A set of stairs descends to a footbridge over the skinny creek.

0.25 Arrive at waterfall. A spur trail leads to a bench for another viewpoint. Retrace your tracks from here or continue to Shovel Point.

0.5 Arrive back at the trailhead.

Built in the early 1900s as a logging camp on the shores of Mic Mac Lake, Tettegouche Camp boasts four historic log cabins for luxe camping digs in the heart of the park.

45 Illgen Falls–Tettegouche State Park

Illgen Falls is no-nonsense beauty, grace, and power all in one, with a historic cabin within earshot of the falls for extended stays.

Waterway: Baptism River
Waterfall beauty: 4
Distance: 0.2 mile out and back
Difficulty: Easy
Hiking time: About 10 minutes
Trail surface: Natural
Other trail users: None
Canine compatibility: Leashed pets allowed

Land status: State park
Fees and permits: Fee required
Maps: Tettegouche State Park map;
USGS Illgen City
Trail contacts: Tettegouche State Park, 5702
Hwy. 61, Silver Bay 55614, (218) 226-6365,
www.dnr.state.mn.us/state_parks/tettegouche

Finding the trailhead: From MN 61, turn north on CR 1 toward Finland. After 1.5 miles, there is a gravel turnout on the left side of the road. Look for the Illgen Falls sign.
Trailhead GPS: N47 21.544' / W91 12.796'

The Hike

Farthest upstream on the Baptism River from Lake Superior is Illgen Falls. Set at the back of a cleft in the gorge, Illgen leaps off a steep escarpment at its crest, free-falling for most of its 40-foot drop before crashing into the tannin-stained plunge pool at its base. The current in the broad pool circulates slowly beneath sheer, bowl-shaped cliffs, curving away from the falls into a wide, V-shaped gap. The whirling water has eroded away the softer rock layers beneath the cliffs, creating overhanging ledges with several dramatic overlooks of the falls, pool, and swiftly flowing river downstream. On the south side of the pool, the cliffs extend steeply upward an additional 40 feet, with fringes of sentinel pines and slender aspen. While the majority of river-related attention in the park often goes to High Falls, Illgen Falls certainly rivals its taller downstream sibling for its simple beauty in a spectacular setting.

In addition to being just plain gorgeous and wonderfully distant from the more crowded environs of the park, Illgen Falls offers overnight accommodations. Tettegouche maintains a furnished, two-bedroom cabin on a bluff within earshot of the falls with a full kitchen, fireplace, deck, and the waterfall just a short walk from the front door. Make reservations through the park for this don't-miss wilderness getaway.

Rich history also runs deep in this area. Illgen Falls shares its name with Illgen City, a small community (proudly proclaiming its population as 4) with important links to the humble beginnings of one of Minnesota's most powerful companies. Like many sites in northern Minnesota, the area around Illgen Falls was explored in the late 1800s and early 1900s by prospectors and investors seeking sources of profitable

Postcard-perfect Ilgen Falls. BRAYDEN MILLS

metals, minerals, or other jackpots hidden below the surface. In 1902 one such group discovered rock near the Baptism River that they believed would make an effective abrasive. The businessmen founded Minnesota Mining and Manufacturing, built a six-story rock crusher near present-day Illgen City, and commenced mining operations. The rock they extracted turned out to be softer than they expected and did not make a good abrasive, and the site was abandoned within a few years. However, the company founders persevered and moved its headquarters to Duluth and then St. Paul, and 3M is now a legendary company known the world over. The crumbled foundations of some of the original 3M buildings remain near the Lake Superior shore not far from Illgen City.

Miles and Directions

0.0 From the parking area, hike toward the river, passing the Illgen Falls cabin on the way. A boardwalk and stairway lead to the crest of the falls. A steep spur trail drops down to river level. Use caution if opting for that route.

0.1 Arrive at river-level view of the falls.

0.2 Arrive back at the trailhead.

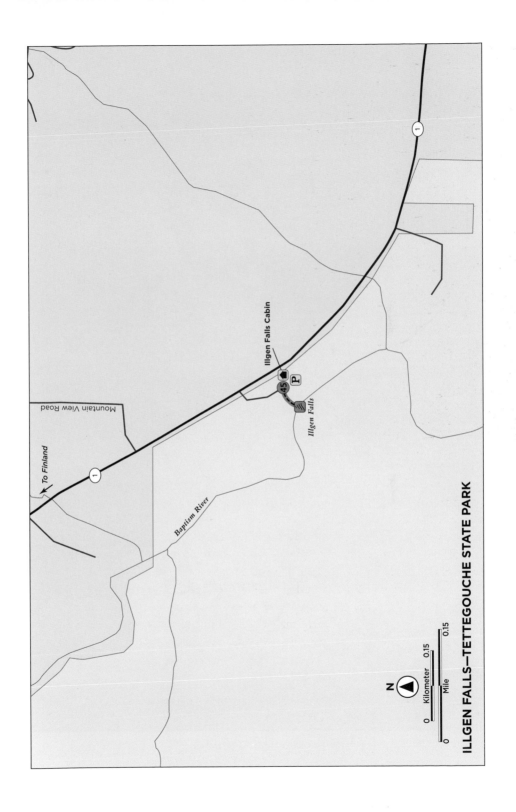

Illgen Falls Cabin

Mountain View Road

To Finland

Baptism River

P

45

Illgen Falls

N

Kilometer   0.15
0

Mile   0.15
0

ILLGEN FALLS—TETTEGOUCHE STATE PARK

Illgen Falls thunders into a black rock gorge. BRAYDEN MILLS

Illgen Falls is radiant on a North Shore summer day. JIM HOFFMAN

Did you know the ubiquitous Post-It® Note was invented by accident by a 3M scientist? Dr. Spencer Silver was busy investigating the world of adhesives for use in airplanes and the like, and happened upon some sticky stuff that would bond lightly, with just the right stick to still allow easy removal. No one at 3M was impressed until Silver's colleague, Art Fry, became frustrated when his bookmarks kept falling out of his church hymnal. Fry used Silver's newfangled glue and never lost another page marker. The two researchers fine-tuned the product and distributed it around their company, to a resounding reception. The iconic yellow color? Also an accident. The lab next door only had scrap paper in yellow. The humble Post-It® Note is now common all over the world, with annual production topping 50 billion.

46 Falls of Manitou River–George H. Crosby Manitou State Park

Crosby Manitou is the most rugged of North Shore state parks, and Minnesota-made for getting way out there on extended hikes and remote backpacking trips. The park's waterfalls highlight the wild vibe of a day in these storied woods.

Waterway: Manitou River
Waterfall beauty: 5
Distance: 2.4-mile loop (0.9 mile one way to The Cascades)
Difficulty: Difficult
Hiking time: About 90 minutes
Trail surface: Natural
Other trail users: None
Canine compatibility: Leashed pets allowed

Land status: State park
Fees and permits: Fee required
Maps: Crosby Manitou State Park map; USGS Little Marais
Trail contacts: c/o Tettegouche State Park, 5702 Hwy. 61, Silver Bay 55614, (218) 226-6365, www.dnr.state.mn.us/state_parks/george_crosby_manitou

Finding the trailhead: From MN 61, follow CR 1 north for 6.5 miles to Finland. Turn right on CR 7 and continue north for 7 miles to the park entrance. Trails start at the parking area on the left, just past the entrance.
Trailhead GPS: N47 28.728' / W91 06.714'

The Hike

Although less than a half dozen crow-fly miles separate Crosby Manitou from the MN 61 traffic buzz, this state park has a rugged, remote spirit full of adventure. The Manitou River, flowing from the lake region way up near Isabella, is one the state's most scenic, and it plunges through Crosby's wilderness environs in a lively parade of cascades and waterfalls. The Superior Hiking Trail (SHT) spends a little time here, and there are 23 miles of additional trails to explore. The hiking is challenging to match the terrain, and the isolated, riverside campsites are a backpacker's delight, along with several unforgettable overlooks of the river valley and Lake Superior.

The park's trailhead area serves as a hub for spokes of trails squiggling off into the woods; it is difficult to resist exploring every one of them. But this hike is all about waterfalls, and the Middle Trail (part of the Superior Hiking Trail in the park) takes us there. (This trail really is smack in the middle of a long loop.) Gorgeous wild-flowers decorate this section of the hike in spring, a colorful prelude to the dramatic main attraction just ahead.

The Cascades is Crosby's celebrity waterfall. A refreshing hike over rolling, rugged terrain gains access to the affair, with bonus events along the way. After crossing

The Manitou River's velvety Cascades. JIM HOFFMAN

boardwalks early on the hike, a spur trail leads to an overlook of the river's valley and surrounding beauteous landscape. Stay alert for wildlife, too. The park is chock-full of a variety of wild critters, including biggies like black bears, timber wolves, moose, and white-tailed deer. A long time ago there were woodland caribou here, as well. Imagine seeing those magnificent animals roaming this very ridge. Regrettably, generations of destructive logging wiped out the caribou's habitat, and they soon vanished from the area.

After some minutes of ogling, keep on truckin' up and down a hill or three, at times with the aid of natural or manufactured stairways, to a hiking and winter-use shelter at the trail's edge. Farther on you pass spur trails heading into the woods and forge ahead on a rocky descent to the junction with the Manitou River Trail. Can you hear the cascades? Go left here and follow the roar along the ridge above the river. A final steep descent on roots and wooden steps delivers you to an outcrop of giant boulders and a head-on view of the Manitou Cascades.

Another postcard-perfect waterfall in the North Country, the Cascades is a long, three-step drop of about 40 feet through a narrow passage of square slabs of rock,

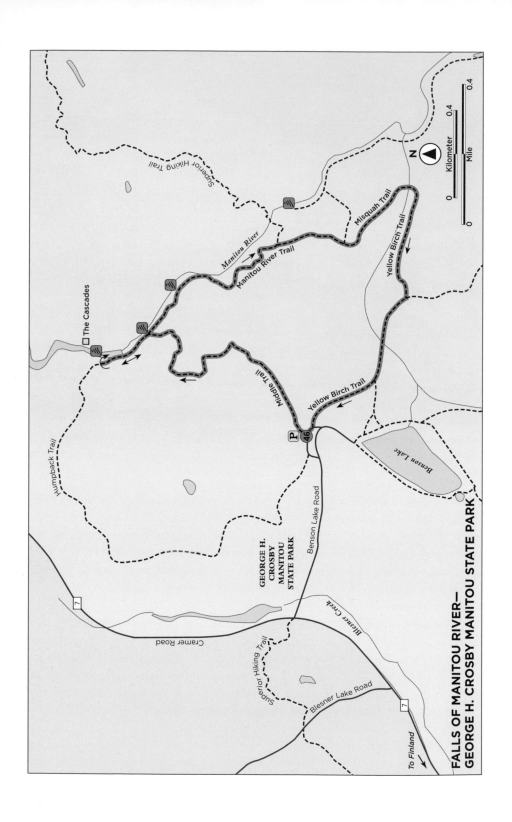

FALLS OF MANITOU RIVER—GEORGE H. CROSBY MANITOU STATE PARK

receding in neatly stacked piles back toward the crest. A palette of green embellishes the scene in a cedar, spruce, and mixed hardwood forest. The river thunders through here in the spring, unfurled like a wavy white carpet, covering nearly the entire river bed in frothy water. In more relaxed times of the year, it's an inviting place to clamber on the boxy boulders and move in a bit closer. Watch your step, though; some of the drops into the river don't give much in the way of second chances before you get wet.

There is one more respectable waterfall on this stretch of the Manitou, followed by a succession of "lesser" cascades that are attractive companions for a hike to outer campsites. Retreat from the Cascades and hike past the Middle Trail junction, following the Manitou River Trail. The path rises steadily to a ridge high above the river and passes campsites 3 and 4. A wooden footbridge appears over a small tributary creek, and from here the trail tilts steeply uphill to a sign for the Superior Hiking Trail. Head left on the SHT, dropping all the way back down to the river and a bridge crossing. Keep an eye out for a spur trail to the left that reveals a great view of a pair of handsome waterfalls, cluttered with pointy boulders that briefly divert the river tumbling toward the bridge. The second waterfall is more of an overgrown rapids dropping about 5 feet over a short stretch of boulders. Stately stands of aspen border the river here, making this an excellent destination for a visit in the dazzling colors of fall.

The trail chugs along far downriver, past numerous small, cascading rapids. Today's route heads back, following the Yellow Birch Trail for a great loop hike to the trailhead. On the way, look aloft for jays, hawks, songbirds of many flavors, and pileated woodpeckers.

Miles and Directions

0.0 From the trailhead, follow the Middle Trail into the rolling woods.

0.5 Junction with Manitou River Trail; turn left.

0.9 Arrive at the Manitou Cascades. Follow the Manitou River Trail to continue the loop past more waterfalls.

1.9 Junction with the Yellow Birch Trail; turn right.

2.4 Arrive back at the trailhead.

Established from its inception to retain its wilderness roots, Crosby Manitou State Park is arguably Minnesota's finest remote backpacking destination. Moose, bears, and wolves take the place of customary park crowds, and Crosby offers only primitive campsites, all requiring a hike to get there. All wild, all the time.

47 Falls of Caribou River

Take one part hike in the north woods, one part stunning waterfall. Mix with an adventuresome spirit and serve in any season. Goes well with wonder and daydreams. Best if experienced multiple times.

Waterway: Caribou River
Waterfall beauty: 4–5
Distance: 1.4 miles out and back (1 mile out and back for Caribou Falls)
Difficulty: Moderate (with a long stairway)
Hiking time: About 1 hour
Trail surface: Natural
Other trail users: None
Canine compatibility: Leashed pets allowed

Land status: State-owned
Fees and permits: No fee required
Maps: Minnesota DNR map;
USGS Little Marais
Trail contacts: Minnesota Department of Natural Resources, 500 Lafayette Rd., St. Paul 55155, (651) 296-6157, dnr.state.mn.us/state_parks/waysides

Finding the trailhead: From Little Marais, follow MN 61 north for 5 miles to Caribou Falls State Wayside at mile marker 70.
Trailhead GPS: N47 27.856' / W91 01.817'

The Hike

There are so many waterfalls in this guide that make the "author favorite" list that I hesitate to keep adding to it, but Caribou Falls is a lock for one of the all-time best. From the humble trailhead tucked in a pocket of woods along MN 61, hikers are treated to another fabulous stroll on the Superior Hiking Trail (SHT), following close to the whispers of the Caribou River. After a short trek the trail heads up a steep climb toward an overlook with stop-in-your-tracks views of Lake Superior. Split off on the spur trail to the left, descending a long stairway to river level at the base of the falls.

The extra-large sandbar spreading into the river makes a great platform for a close-up meeting with the falls. Caribou is a delight as it enters a split in the steep gorge high above, erupting through the rock and splaying wider in a long, 35-foot slide of rugged, stepped ledges to the round pool at your feet. Lush green foliage of shrubbery and noble forest colors the tops of the gorge's black rock. Way up there, the trees look small enough to haul into the living room and decorate for Christmas. At river level during high water, the roar of the waterfall's long white sheets echoes from the high cliff walls, and it can be difficult to hear your buddy sing praise to the beauty of this place. At more relaxed times of the year, stretching out on this sandbar and listening to the spellbinding sounds of the falls is paradise found.

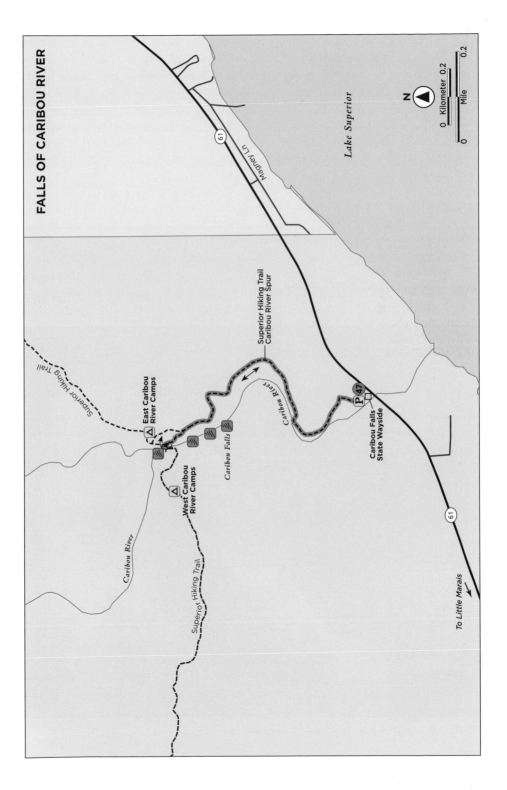

FALLS OF CARIBOU RIVER

Head back up the stairs and up the big hill on the trail to the overlook to ogle the view. How's that for a reward for your efforts? Best of all, there are more photogenic waterfalls just upstream. Hike along the SHT, with the river's urgent clamor below. Two more falls appear, resplendent from high on the ridge. A short way farther is a bridge over the river with a fourth waterfall cascading beneath it into a skinny, ragged gorge, and yet another is up from the bridge, embracing an island of rocks in two frolicking streams.

The trailhead is only about a 30-minute, downhill hike, so this is a good spot to take a breather and linger a bit.

Miles and Directions

0.0   From the trailhead, follow the path along the river.

0.5   Arrive at a spur trail with lots of stairs leading down to river level and a sweet view of Caribou Falls.

0.6   Pass three more waterfalls with views from the ridge but no access to river level.

Caribou Falls fans into a pretty veil. JIM HOFFMAN

Caribou Falls cascades into a rugged gorge washed with emerald green cedar. BRAYDEN MILLS

0.7   Arrive at a bridge over the river and another waterfall sailing into a narrow gorge. Yet another falls shows its best stuff just upstream from the bridge. Retrace your steps to return to the trailhead.

1.4   Arrive back at the trailhead.

Caribou Falls State Wayside is one of nine included in Minnesota's state park system. These waysides are on acreage too small to be considered "grown-up" state parks, but with enough stay-awhile features to make them great stops to do just that. Five of these waysides are found along the North Shore.

48 Two Island Falls

A ghost town mystique and palpable ore-refining history add to the allure of this unexpectedly scenic cascade.

Waterway: Two Island River
Waterfall beauty: 3.5
Distance: 0.4 mile out and back
Difficulty: Easy
Hiking time: About 20 minutes
Trail surface: Natural
Other trail users: None

Canine compatibility: Leashed pets allowed
Land status: Public
Fees and permits: No fee required
Maps: USGS Little Marais
Trail contacts: Cook County Visitors Bureau, 116 W. Hwy. 61, Grand Marais 55604, (218) 387-2188, www.visitcookcounty.com

Finding the trailhead: From Schroeder, follow MN 61 south for 2 miles. Near mile marker 77, park on the side of the road or in the gravel parking area on the lake side.
Trailhead GPS: N47 31.434' / W90 55.564'

The Hike

The falls of the Two Island River provide picturesque falls in an unusual setting—they are the only falls in Minnesota's Arrowhead region flanked by a mammoth ore-refining environment. The upper falls begin as a tumbling cascade pouring out of a forest of birch into a narrow cleft of rock. After cascading over several smaller drops, the water plunges freely over a 20-foot falls into a bowl-shaped pool. From the pool the river passes under a railroad trestle and gently tumbles toward Taconite Harbor and Lake Superior. The faint trail from the upper falls wanders back down toward the highway to the smaller lower falls. The lower falls begin as gentle cascades, angling into two sharp turns to a wide, flat ledge and finally pouring over a final, 2-foot drop to an oval-shaped pool. From here the river makes its way beneath the highway through two huge drainage pipes. Downstream are smaller cascades with easy access to the middle of the river, with a view of the highway bridge and the culverts. They look like big eyes beneath a crown of cement eyebrows.

Like a few other waterfalls included in this book, this one has undergone man-made alterations. However, in this case the modifications are less about the waterfall itself, and much more on the surrounding lands. The immense taconite plant required roads for big trucks and lines for trains, and lots of room to make giant piles of iron ore. The railroad grade providing access to Taconite Harbor for iron ore trains chugging in from the Vermilion and Mesabi Iron Ranges not only spans the Two Island River, but also slices through the hard igneous rock surrounding the falls.

Two Island River's upper falls. JIM HOFFMAN

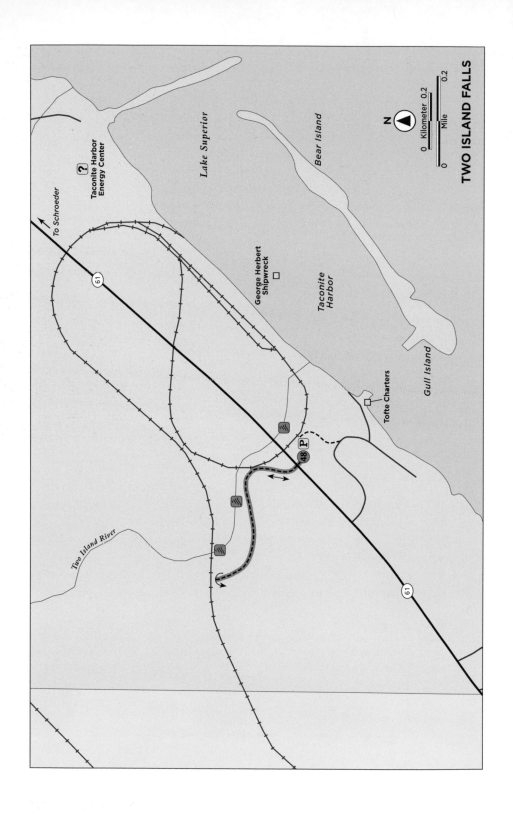

TWO ISLAND FALLS

The Two Island River zigs and zags. JIM HOFFMAN

In spite of its harsh appearance, the Taconite Harbor plant and present-day ghost town offer a glimpse into the not-so-recent past. The plant was an active refiner of crude iron ore into taconite pellets for use in making steel and other iron-derived products, and the harbor was regularly occupied by huge, seafaring ore ships taking on thousands of tons of taconite.

All that remains of the town are crumbling foundations, abandoned streets reclaimed by determined foliage, and remnant relics of a life gone by.

Miles and Directions

0.0. From the trailhead at the highway, hike the trail through a striking birch and conifer forest along the river to the upper falls. Look for cool potholes in the rocks below the highway before heading upstream.

0.2 Turn around at the upper falls.

0.4 Arrive back at the trailhead.

An emerald green backdrop on the river. JIM HOFFMAN

Here and gone. In classic boomtown style, the compact community of Taconite Harbor bloomed seemingly overnight—twenty-two spic-and-span homes for workers at Erie Mining Company, which kept a fever pace refining and shipping around 10 million tons of taconite pellets annually. The early 1980s ushered in hard times, and in less than ten years the mining industry stumbled, forcing the shutdown of the facility and exodus of Taconite Harbor's proud families.

49 Cross River Falls

The Cross River sails down beneath the bridge in a torrent of froth and speed. Because of its significant height and consistently strong flow, this long, steep cascade is one of the most attractive falls along the North Shore.

Waterway: Cross River
Waterfall beauty: 4
Distance: 100 yards out and back
Difficulty: Easy
Hiking time: About 5 minutes
Trail surface: Paved, with natural spur trails
Other trail users: None

Canine compatibility: Leashed pets allowed
Land status: Public
Fees and permits: No fee required
Maps: Schroeder area maps; USGS Schroeder
Trail contacts: Cook County Visitors Bureau, 116 W. Hwy. 61, Grand Marais 55604, (218) 387-2188, www.visitcookcounty.com

Finding the trailhead: Park in the lot on the west side of MN 61, across from the Cross River Heritage Center in Schroeder. The waterfall is in clear view directly from the Highway 61 bridge at the Cross River Falls Wayside.
Trailhead GPS: N47 32.634' / W90 53.843'

The Hike

Getting to this waterfall is simply a matter of standing on the Highway 61 bridge in Schroeder. From the bridge-top vantage point, the river meets a gigantic boulder slicing the river in two, then reconnects on the downstream side blazing like an arrow under the bridge. The best view is at the base of the falls, where the river falls into a deep gorge adorned with towering cedar trees. The waterfall cascades at the top into a narrow crevice and then blasts out the downstream side, hastily making its way over a second tier of rock to a deep pool. Two enormous cedars stand as gate-keepers on both sides of the waterfall. The pool flows over a secondary falls, where the river then continues through the scenic gorge to Lake Superior.

An interesting side trip nearby is Father Baraga's Cross, just north of Schroeder. Follow the signs and dirt road from MN 61 to the lakeshore. A large granite cross is perched on a knoll at the water's edge. Father Frederic Baraga was an Indian missionary, born in 1797 in Slovenia. He traveled by canoe and steamship in the summer months and by snowshoe in winter, traversing 80,000 square miles of Minnesota's woods to visit remote Indian settlements. In 1843 he and guide Louis Gaudin were caught in a furious storm while crossing Lake Superior in a small boat from Madeline Island on the lake's south shore. The story goes that Baraga prayed throughout the storm, assuring Gaudin that God wouldn't let them die. The gale blew the boat toward a treacherous shoal of rocks along the North Shore, and it is said a huge wave

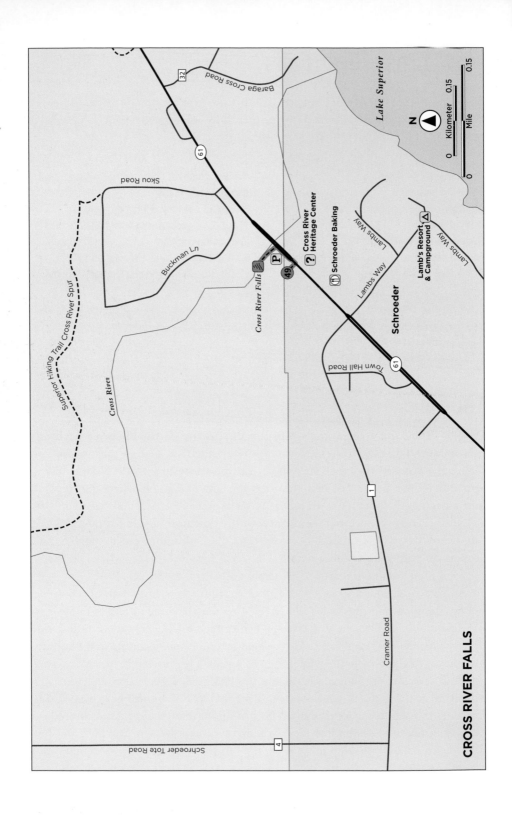

CROSS RIVER FALLS

Cross River cascades in full flight. JIM HOFFMAN

picked the boat up and set it gently down in a pool at the mouth of a river, where they reached land safe and sound.

Later the men erected a wooden cross—since replaced by the present granite model—to mark the spot of what they considered to be a miracle. The Cross River is named for the incident.

In addition to Baraga's Cross, the Cross River State Wayside provides a 2,500-acre outdoor playground, including sections of the Superior Hiking Trail and North Shore State Trail. Two backcountry campsites are available along the SHT within the wayside boundaries.

Miles and Directions

0.0 Walk to the bridge for a dead-on view of the falls. It's about 100 yards from the parking lot to the falls.

50 Falls of Temperance River— Temperance River State Park

Put this one on your North Shore bucket list. The Temperance River gorge and surrounding trails feel like walking through Middle Earth. Bring the kids and pretend they're hobbits in this magical lakeside park.

Waterway: Temperance River
Waterfall beauty: 4–5
Distance: 1.8 miles out and back
Difficulty: Easy to moderate
Hiking time: About 40 minutes, but plan on extra for exploring
Trail surface: Paved and natural
Other trail users: None on river trail; multi-interest users on Gitchi-Gami Trail

Canine compatibility: Leashed pets allowed
Land status: State park
Fees and permits: Fee required
Maps: Temperance River State Park map; USGS Schroeder, USGS Tofte
Trail contacts: Temperance River State Park, 7620 W. Hwy. 61, Box 33, Schroeder 55613, (218) 663-7476, www.dnr.state.mn.us/state_parks/temperance_river

Finding the trailhead: From Schroeder, go 2 miles north on MN 61 to the river bridge. Ample parking is available in a turnout on the west side of the highway, just before the park entrance. **Trailhead GPS:** N47 33.310' / W90 52.419'

The Hike

The sign at the trailhead announces seven scenic overlooks along this trail that highlight rocky river gorges, hidden waterfalls, and cauldrons. An intriguing prologue, indeed, and we haven't taken a single step away from the highway. Numerous waterfalls and cascades are included in the park's collection along this lower section of the Temperance River, and you can find five favorites here. It is difficult, however, to go exploring with such a dramatic scene right beneath the Highway 61 bridge. Two trails on either side of the river delve into stunning, rugged scenery of plump cedar trees, towering white pines, and white and yellow birch. The trees hug the edges of a craggy gorge with hard angles and vertical walls lined with lightning bolt cracks. A waterfall small in size but loud in voice crashes into a deep pool in the gorge and makes a beeline to Lake Superior. A nifty footbridge crosses the river just below the zigzag gorge for great views in both directions. The trails continue to short, rocky bluffs and to the lakeshore for splendiferous vistas of the big lake. This is almost enough to make a day of it right there.

The Temperance River is called a "wild and violent river," with good measure. The Temperance does not glide gently around a bend of chattering riffles; it announces itself with guns blazing, thundering through these canyons in angry cracks

The wildly scenic Temperance River Gorge. BRAYDEN MILLS

of rapids, with unimaginable force pounding into colossal boulders and sluicing cliffs of shadowy basalt. Thousands of years of this relentless battle of water and rock created huge potholes in the soft lava of the river bed, and the potholes grew and eventually succumbed to the watery assault, collapsing into the next pothole, and the one after that, to create the deep, slender gorge you see today.

One of the spoils of this primeval skirmish is the series of waterfalls on the river in a short section of the gorge between Lake Superior and higher ground upstream. The first treasure is Hidden Falls, concealed way back in a dark, deep cave of the gorge. Ragged profiles of vertical gray rock, crowned with green cedar trees, guard the cave from close inspection, but the waterfall is visible through a narrow window in the rock. The falls flow smoothly into an unseen pool and then snake through a skinny crack in the rocks.

The path follows the river to a collection of overlooks and climbs a flight of stone steps, like an aged stairway through Tolkien's Mines of Moria. Similar to Gooseberry Falls State Park and many other locations in northern Minnesota, these steps, trail corridors, and creative sitting areas were crafted by gifted artisans of the Civilian Conservation Corps.

The Temperance River's upper falls. JIM HOFFMAN

Hiking tabletop rocks above the gorge.
BRAYDEN MILLS

Hidden Falls. JIM HOFFMAN

Farther along the trail is a head-on look at the next waterfall. We dubbed this one Fissure Falls for the river's persistence in finding the skinny crack in a solid wall of rock, so as not to interrupt its journey. Whiskers of deep green moss and blotches of rusty lichen cling to rocks, while suds of foam float around on the small pool below. A small rise in the trail leads across the Gitchi-Gami State Trail, a fantastic multiuse recreation path that, when completed, will wander through nearly 90 miles of stunning North Country scenery from Two Harbors to Grand Marais. From the Gitchi's bridge over the river, and from one of the advertised overlooks, is a closer view of Fissure Falls shooting through the rocks.

A short trek up the trail (hiking now on the hallowed Superior Hiking Trail [SHT]), past some of the most beautiful, unadulterated North Country land in the entire Arrowhead region, is another postcard waterfall. The gorge opens up and exposes cliff walls like the teeth of a great beast, with a white tongue of water and foam hissing at the center of its blackened maw. This is White Falls, named for the top to bottom color of the roaring rapids and the frothy bubble bath of foam at its base. Another overlook provides a dead-ahead view of this falls and surrounding wild forest.

One more waterfall lies in wait before the SHT gradually leans away from the river toward Carlton Peak, a 1,526-foot hill with knock-your-boots-off views of

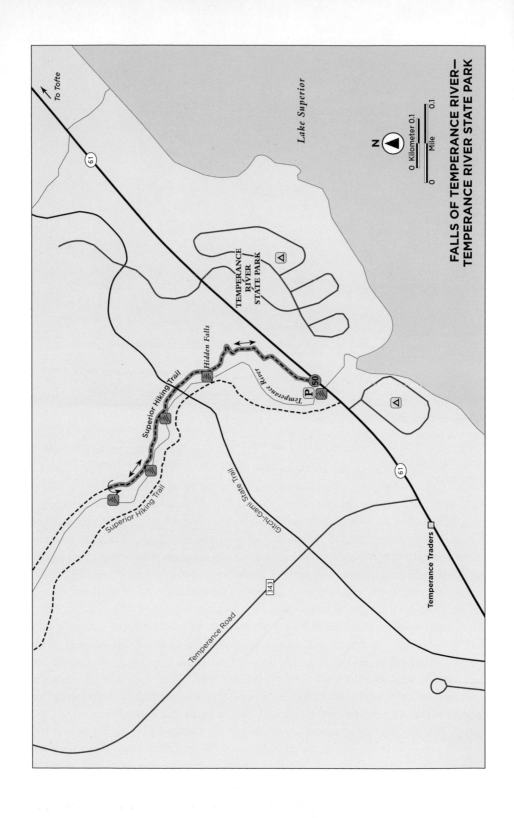

**FALLS OF TEMPERANCE RIVER—
TEMPERANCE RIVER STATE PARK**

A trail bridge over the river gorge. JIM HOFFMAN

Lake Superior and its grand shore. This falls is a pretty little cascade, considerably tamer than its downstream brethren, but still radiating enough allure to hold you riveted to its rugged grace. Author-named Echo Falls makes an initial surge into the side of a small cliff, then angles a sharp right turn into a dark plunge pool, where it eddies around a bit and sneaks through a half-circle opening in the gorge walls.

Temperance River State Park hosts all of this amazing scenery and tops it off with an excellent campground an agate's throw from the waters of Superior. This is a highly recommended, author-favorite, don't-miss stop on any North Shore visit.

Miles and Directions

0.0 From the trailhead, follow the path into the river gorge.

0.15 Arrive at Hidden Falls.

0.18 Cross the Gitchi-Gami State Trail.

0.9 Arrive at Echo Falls. Hike on to reach Carlton Peak, or retrace your tracks to the trailhead.

1.8 Arrive back at the trailhead.

The counterpart to the unimaginable forces from a billion or so years ago that formed the Temperance River's gorge of igneous rock is an equally impressive feat in the other direction. Nearby Carlton Peak, the 1,526-foot knob in the park's northeastern corner, is made of a jumble of super-hard anorthosite, originating in and heaved up by fiery hot molten lava from miles below the surface.

51 Onion River Falls

Flowing through a popular wayside stop along MN 61, the Onion River's waterfalls are among the prettiest in the state, with an especially scenic bonus hike thrown in.

Waterway: Onion River
Waterfall beauty: 3.5-4
Distance: 0.8 mile out and back
Difficulty: Moderate
Hiking time: About 20 minutes
Trail surface: Natural
Other trail users: None
Canine compatibility: Leashed pets allowed

Land status: State-owned
Fees and permits: No fee required
Maps: Minnesota DNR map; USGS Tofte
Trail contacts: Minnesota Department of Natural Resources, 500 Lafayette Rd., St. Paul 55155, (651) 296-6157, dnr.state.mn.us/state_parks/waysides

Finding the trailhead: From Tofte, head north on MN 61 for 4 miles to the Ray Berglund State Wayside. The trail starts at the historical marker.
Trailhead GPS: N47 36.551' / W90 46.157'

The Hike

While the dramatic displays of falls on other rivers crash into your memories like liquid fireworks, the Onion River's falls are more of a soothing slide. There are two options to reach the falls, one in the woods high above the river and the other right in the river, given cooperative water levels. The high road starts at the west end of the wayside parking area, where a flight of wooden steps climbs a steep bank into dense woods along the top of the gorge. A dirt path forges through vibrant foliage for approximately 0.4 mile to a narrow spur trail leading to an area of open, exposed rock at the base of the upper cascade and the crest of the lower cascade. This route is the best choice when water levels are high.

If the water is low, it's fun to follow the creek bed from the parking lot, scrambling upstream over a congested bed of smooth river pebbles and ragged, basketball-size boulders to the base of the waterfall. The creek is quiet on this downstream stretch from the falls, with a few riffles here and there skirting past vertical slabs of rock flushed green with moss and algae. The upper portion of the falls is partially obscured from view from the base, due to the impressive height of the cascade, but it is still a handsome scene.

The main attraction of Onion River Falls is that it's another hidden North Shore gem, infrequently visited but uniquely beautiful. The river is a small, narrow, tannin-stained stream that gurgles gently through a forest of primarily second-growth birch and thick underbrush. At the crest of the cascade, the river spreads out into a wide, shallow film of white that pours over a giant, two-tiered step of curving rock, like

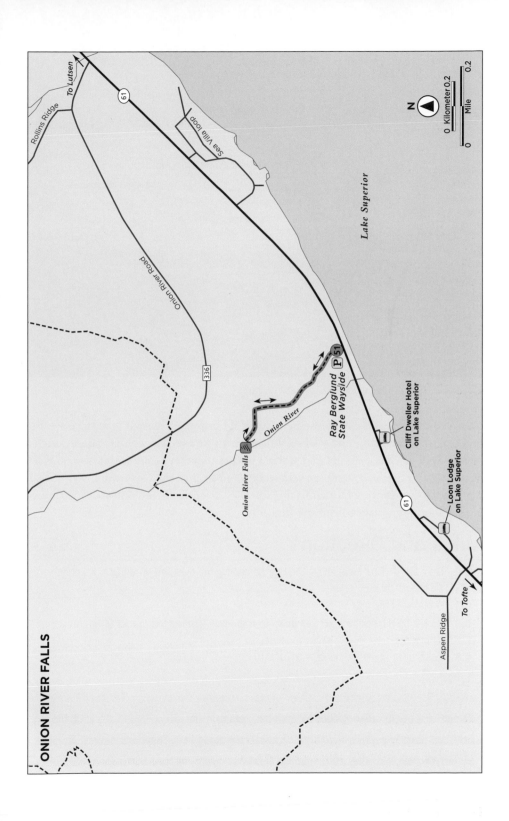

ONION RIVER FALLS

The lower slide of Onion River Falls. BRAYDEN MILLS

one of those big slides at amusement parks. The initial waterfall way up on top is more of a vertical drop, and then it sluices down in a translucent cascade through a secluded, high-walled gorge. The water squishes together again at the center of the descent, collecting in a small pool, then fans out in lacy veils over the lower slide. It is a very relaxing setting hidden in this shadowy gorge, and feels remote even though within shouting distance from the highway.

Miles and Directions

0.0 From the parking area, follow the trail paralleling the river and up a flight of wooden stairs.

0.2 Overlook of the falls.

0.4 Go left on the narrow spur trail down to river level. Retrace your tracks to return to the trailhead.

0.8 Arrive back at the trailhead.

Named for a conservation-minded St. Paul businessman with strong ties to the area, the Ray Berglund State Wayside is a popular highway stop along Lake Superior's shores. Travelers, anglers, cyclists, and other users frequent this lakeside area on their North Shore adventures.

52 Upper Falls—Poplar River

A stalwart North Shore destination for generations, Lutsen Resort has it all for life-list memories. Neighboring Lutsen Mountains is the stuff of legend for skiers and mountain bikers, and the Poplar River flows right through it all, complete with easy-access hiking trails and photo-op historical bridges.

Waterway: Poplar River
Waterfall beauty: 5
Distance: 0.8 mile out and back
Difficulty: Easy
Hiking time: About 20 minutes
Trail surface: Paved and natural
Other trail users: None

Canine compatibility: Leashed pets allowed
Land status: Lutsen Resort
Fees and permits: No fee required
Maps: Various resort maps; USGS Lutsen
Trail ccntacts: Lutsen Resort,
5700 W. Hwy. 61, Lutsen 55612,
(218) 206-8157, www.lutsenresort.com

Finding the trailhead: From MN 61, turn north onto CR 5 (Ski Hill Road) and head up to the ski area. Look for the gondola parking area. Hike the gravel road to the start of the trail. A Superior Hiking Trail sign leads the way to the South Oberg Trail and then to the falls.
Trailhead GPS: N47 39.967' / W90 43.146'

The Hike

Lutsen Mountain Resort, one of Minnesota's premier destinations for frolicking in the great outdoors, is fortunate to have the gorgeous Poplar River flowing through its grounds. Lutsen's outdoors are legendary. There is highlight-reel grandeur in every direction, and activities for everyone in every season—especially the self-propelled variety, like mountain biking that rivals the big mountains out west, the best skiing in the Midwest, golf, cross-country skiing, and hiking. All this in a setting of the high, rolling hills of the Sawtooth Mountains, enchanting forest, and the incomparable backdrop of Lake Superior. You will likely have trouble just passing beyond the bustle of fun at the main resort. Top-shelf mountain bikes await rental for two-wheeling through the woods. The Hiking Center supplies the goods and scoop for strolling around the resort's trails, or disappearing on a multiday trek. Ride the Mountain Tram to the top of Moose Mountain for unforgettable aerial views of the North Shore, or hop a chairlift up to Eagle Mountain and sail down the Alpine Slide. There is also horseback riding, wildlife viewing, and great grub and live entertainment at Papa Charlie's.

For a closer look at the twisty ribbon of the Poplar River, and especially its dramatic waterfall, just follow the road past the resort complex to the South Oberg trailhead. A gradual descent through pine, aspen, and maple woods is a nice prelude, and the clamor of the falls gets louder with each step. At the bottom of the hill is a

UPPER FALLS—POPLAR RIVER

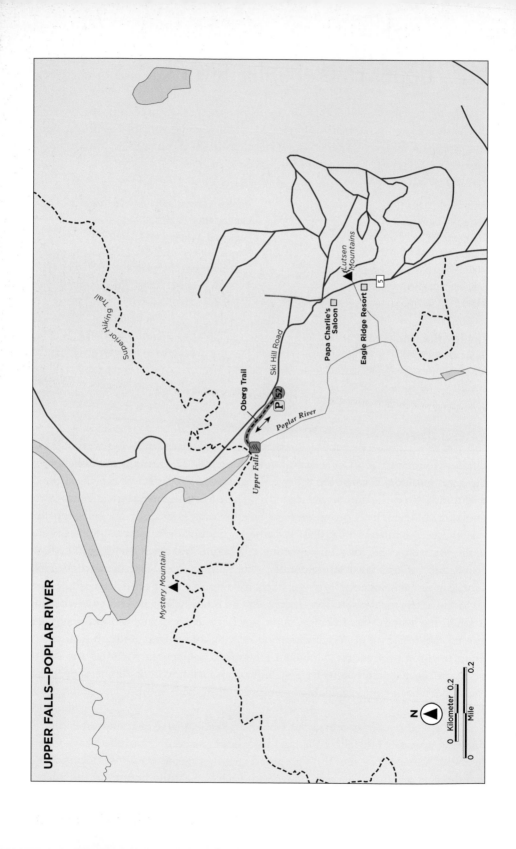

Lutsen's dramatic Upper Falls. BRAYDEN MILLS

bridge over the river, and the waterfall roars below. The river approaches a rapid drop in elevation in a funnel of this rugged gorge. Right below the bridge, the river blasts through a wedge of huge boulders and plummets out of sight into the wider gorge below, on its way to Lake Superior. The view from farther down the steep, rocky walls is amazing. This is a dazzling waterfall, thundering at full volume over several tiers of massive rocks. It is a powerful sight that speaks loudly of the beauty of this special area. The waterfall slides nearly 50 feet and reveals many battles between the inexorable pounding from the river and the enduring defense of obstinate glacial detritus. A battalion of miniature waterfalls squirt from fissures and chutes in the rock, creating their own skirmishes in the larger fracas.

Below the waterfall the river pools briefly and then ambles through a breathlessly scenic landscape of dense foliage and rocky valley walls past the bases of the ski runs and fluttering flags of golf course greens to the big lake beyond.

Miles and Directions

0.0 Follow the South Oberg Trail through the woods, descending gradually toward the river.

0.4 Arrive at the river and waterfall. Return the same way.

0.8 Arrive back at the trailhead.

53 Lower Falls—Poplar River

Linger in the history of Minnesota's oldest resort, with hypnotic Lake Superior views outside and good grub inside.

Waterway: Poplar River
Waterfall beauty: 5
Distance: 100 yards or so
Difficulty: Easy
Hiking time: About 5 minutes
Trail surface: Natural
Other trail users: None

Canine compatibility: Leashed pets allowed
Land status: Lutsen Resort
Fees and permits: No fee required
Maps: Various resort maps; USGS Lutsen
Trail contacts: Lutsen Resort,
5700 W. Hwy. 61, Lutsen 55612,
(218) 206-8157, www.lutsenresort.com

Finding the trailhead: From MN 61, turn south onto Resort Road and follow it to the east side of the lodge at Lutsen Resort. A sign for the River Trail leads to the waterfall.
Trailhead GPS: N47 38.192' / W90 42.464'

The Hike

The lower falls on the Poplar River are on the grounds of Lutsen Resort, Minnesota's oldest resort, with a 100-year history of entertaining generations of visitors. A Swedish immigrant named Charles Axel Nelson was attracted, and rightly so, to the outstanding beauty of the North Shore and decided to build a home here. He named it "Lutsen," and history tells us that as his home grew in size to accommodate his family, travelers in the area routinely stopped in to rest. Pretty soon, word spread that the Nelson place was a mighty fine refuge to catch a nap and gobble a hearty meal, and before long travelers came to stay while enjoying the north woods. And so began a long tradition of providing a treasured North Shore haven for visitors.

How often do you get to stroll across a covered bridge these days? The historic sheltered spans of yore are rapidly disappearing, but Lutsen has two of them right on the grounds! Both bridges extend across the Poplar River, one at the mouth emptying into Lake Superior, the other a short distance upstream. The short River Trail leads as promised to the bridge and a small but spirited waterfall directly below. The river cuts through a narrow slice in a huge hunk of dark gray rock, and while it only falls about 5 feet, it does so with verve that belies its small stature. At the bottom of the main tumble, the river bends gently left and right through mellow cascades toward the second bridge and the big lake. The bridges and the grounds at the lodge are fantastic, made even more so by a long history of family pride and tradition.

Lower Falls at Lutsen Resort. BRAYDEN MILLS ▶

LOWER FALLS—POPLAR RIVER

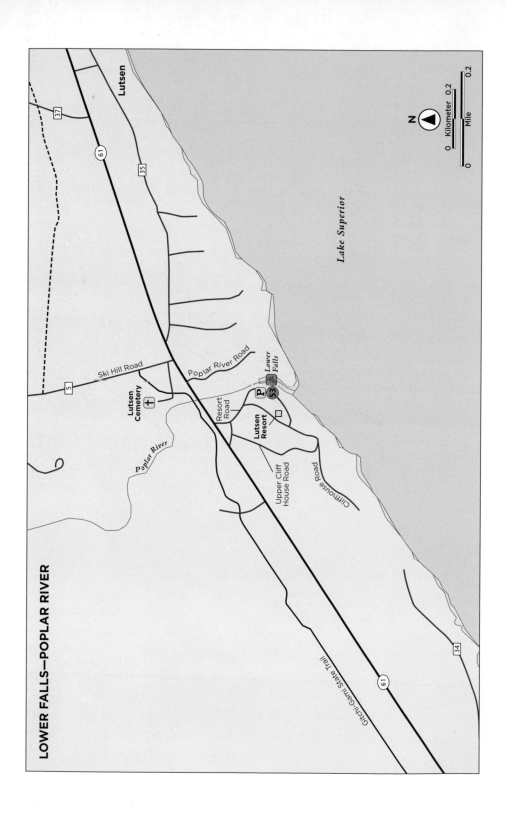

Top: *Footbridge and aged river shack at Lower Falls.* BRAYDEN MILLS
Bottom: *Covered bridge at Lower Falls.* JIM HOFFMAN

Miles and Directions

0.0 From the trailhead at the lodge, follow the River Trail sign, descending on the trail and a handful of steps to the riverbank and a great view of the falls. It's about 100 yards from the trailhead to the falls.

Bonus points: This area is great fun to explore. Wander the trails to the mouth of the river and the sprawling beach for amazing lake views and quality relaxing time.

Lutsen Mountains is a spectacular launch pad for extended hiking adventures. Right from the Poplar Falls bridge, head out in either direction on the Superior Hiking Trail for long miles. Take the tram up Mystery Mountain for faraway views of Lake Superior and inland forest. Untold miles of woodland trails and forest roads also wind through the area.

54 Thompson Falls

Venture inland to the wild recesses of the Superior National Forest and upper stretches of the Cascade River for some quality alone time with secluded and handsome Thompson Falls.

Waterway: Cascade River
Waterfall beauty: 5
Distance: 0.3 mile out and back
Difficulty: Easy
Hiking time: About 10 minutes
Trail surface: Natural
Other trail users: None
Canine compatibility: Leashed pets allowed

Land status: Superior National Forest
Fees and permits: No fee required
Maps: National Forest maps; USGS Mark Lake
Trail contacts: Superior National Forest, Gunflint Ranger District, 2020 W. Hwy. 61, Grand Marais 55604, (218) 387-1750, www.fs.usda.gov/detail/superior/about-forest/offices

Finding the trailhead: From MN 61 in Lutsen, follow Caribou Trail (CR 4) north for 17 miles, all the way to its end at the junction with FR 153, known locally as "The Grade." Turn right and head east for 2.4 miles to FR 158 (Bally Creek Road) and turn right again. About 0.2 mile south is a turnout and sign for Thompson Falls on the right. The trail to the falls leaves from the parking area.
Trailhead GPS: N47 51.608' / W90 32.686'

The Hike

Thompson Falls is one of Minnesota's most secluded waterfalls, and one of the longest. The rocky trail from the road leads into dense stands of spruce, white pine, birch, balsam, and aspen. Hiking through this kind of stately forest never gets old, does it? For me, half the fun of waterfalling is hanging out with the trees.

The trail wanders past a wide, marshy section of the river and then heads toward the roar of the falls. It's an easy hike with access to the base of the waterfall, and lots of places to explore. Thompson Falls blasts over the crest and unfurls wide like a river delta, with a gaggle of mini falls along the fringe. In times of gentler flow, it's fun to rock-hop out into the river and feel the water curl past.

Below the falls, the river bends and splits at an island of trees, drifts into another bulbous marsh, and continues its winding trip toward Lake Superior.

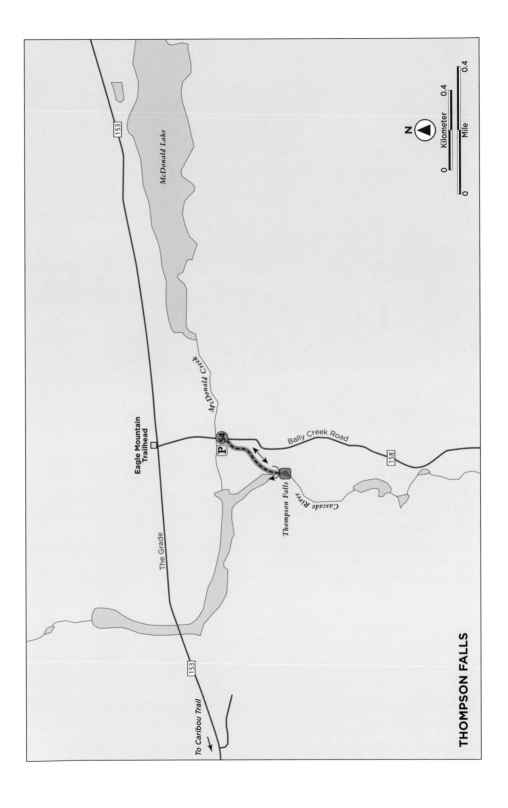

THOMPSON FALLS

The Cascade River unfurls at Thompson Falls. BRAYDEN MILLS

Miles and Directions

0.0 From the parking turnout, follow the rocky path into the woods, passing a marshy stretch of the river.

0.1 Arrive at the falls. Various routes lead to the base of the big cascade, and this is a wonderful place to explore and linger. Return the same way.

0.3 Arrive back at the trailhead.

55 Cascade Falls and The Cascades–Cascade River State Park

Intimate trails, aged cedars, waterfalls, and a fantasy-world rocky gorge will leave you spellbound. Settle in and stay awhile.

Waterway: Cascade River
Waterfall beauty: 5
Distance: 0.5 mile out and back
Difficulty: Easy to moderate (with stairs)
Hiking time: About 30 minutes
Trail surface: Natural
Other trail users: None
Canine compatibility: Leashed pets allowed
Land status: State park

Fees and permits: Fee required if entering the park area; no fee to hike from highway parking trailhead
Maps: Cascade River State Park map; USGS Deer Yard Lake
Trail contacts: Cascade River State Park, 3481 W. Hwy. 61, Lutsen 55612, (218) 387-3053, www.dnr.state.mn.us/state_parks/cascade_river

Finding the trailhead: Cascade River State Park is located 10 miles southwest of Grand Marais on MN 61. Park in the lot along the highway, just south of the river.
Trailhead GPS: N47 42.422' / W90 31.453'

The Hike

Here is another outrageously beautiful state park in the North Shore collection, with vibrant forests and enchanting rock formations in the Cascade River gorge. The park boasts two handsome waterfalls within easy reach of the highway, and more just a short, scenic hike upstream. There are also many miles of hiking trails in the park and neighboring lands in and around the Sawtooth Mountains.

Cascade Falls tumbles 25 feet into a deep crevasse just a short hike upstream from Lake Superior. It looks like a giant spoonful of rock was scooped out, leaving behind a tightly curved cirque and shadowy alcove behind the falls. The scene is embellished with a crowd of towering, deep green cedar trees and luxuriant mosses draped on the dark rock of the cliff walls. The brown color of the water—a product of tannic acid in the current—and white, puffy foam from the roiling rapids make it easy to imagine the river as a giant root beer float with never-ending refills.

Keep an eye out for some of the critters that have chosen to take up residence in this wonderful place. White-tailed deer, of course, are plentiful in the park's environs, as are foxes, pine martens, black bears, and wolves, to name only a few. Musically inclined songbirds also thrive here, as well as majestic hawk and eagle species.

Elegant Cascade Falls. JIM HOFFMAN

Cascade Falls plunges into a black rock gorge. BRAYDEN MILLS

The Cascades

Only a short hike upstream from Cascade Falls, up and down wooden stairways that hug the rolling terrain, is a triple-decker treat where the river dances down three drops in a tight section of the gorge. Craggy walls with fragrant cedar and spruce direct the river in a sidestep boogie right, left, then right-left again as the frothy current skedaddles toward the larger falls below. These are The Cascades, a mesmerizing display of North Country magic that invites extended lingering.

It's not over yet. A short hike upstream leads to more waterfalls. Rugged stone steps descend past a mossy rock ledge to the river. Scores of pungent cedars shade a series of lively falls and a placid pool. There is more water falling farther upriver, with challenging flights of steps and wood-plank bridges. Check it out or head back here for the return to the trailhead.

After ogling the falls, hikers can disappear into the tangle of trails in and around the park. There are 18 miles of dedicated hiking trails in the state park itself, and 17 more of cross-country ski trails. The magnificent Superior Hiking Trail parallels the river on both sides and delves far inland for an unforgettable day hike. Try Lookout Mountain, just west of the waterfalls, for its promised, far-off views of the Sawtooths and Lake Superior. The park also has several backcountry campsites, a gorgeous campground, and a fun shoreline trail with picnic sites.

A sudsy pool below an impromptu log bridge. BRAYDEN MILLS

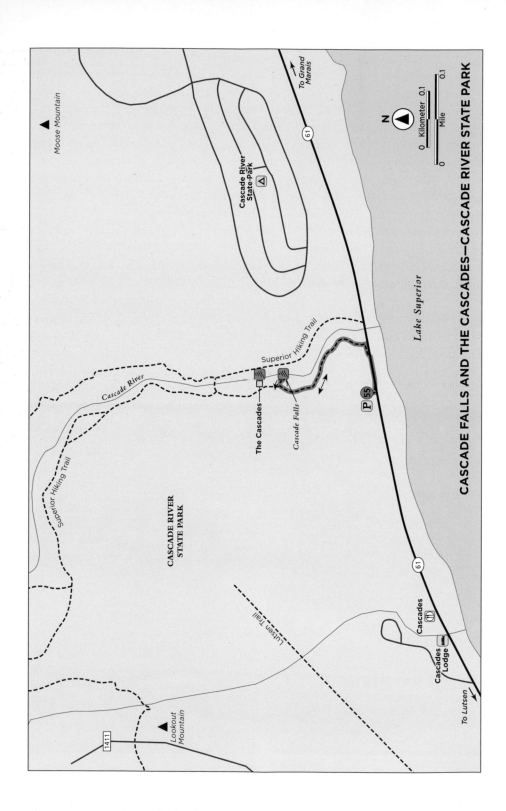

CASCADE FALLS AND THE CASCADES—CASCADE RIVER STATE PARK

The Cascades stairstep through a funnel of craggy cliffs. BRAYDEN MILLS

Miles and Directions

0.0 From the trailhead, simply follow the path about 100 yards to the waterfall. Continue upstream for more falls.

0.2 Arrive at views of The Cascades. Only a few dozen more steps upriver lead to more water-falls. When you've had your fill, retrace your track the same way, or wander a bit farther for new scenery on the trail on the other side of the river.

0.5 Arrive back at the trailhead.

The black basalt rock forming Cascade River's gorge looks like an impenetrable, immovable mass of mightiness. Stand on the park's footbridge over the river, however, and you realize the real force is the water. The bridge trembles with the ferocity of the river's current as it inexorably cuts and grinds and carves through the billion-year-old rock.

56 Hidden Falls—Cascade River

Get crowd-free splendor upstream from Cascade River State Park at this aptly named waterfall.

Waterway: Cascade River
Waterfall beauty: 5
Distance: 0.8 mile out and back
Difficulty: Easy
Hiking time: About 30 minutes
Trail surface: Natural
Other trail users: None
Canine compatibility: Leashed pets allowed

Land status: Public
Fees and permits: No fee required
Maps: Cascade River State Park map; USGS Deer Yard Lake
Trail contacts: Cascade River State Park, 3481 W. Hwy. 61, Lutsen 55612, (218) 387-3053, www.dnr.state.mn.us/state_parks/cascade_river

Finding the trailhead: From MN 61, 0.8 mile northeast of Cascade River State Park, head northeast on CR 7 for 1.9 miles to CR 44. Turn left (north) and go 0.5 mile to CR 45. Go left and in 2.5 miles look for a parking area at the Cascade River bridge.
Trailhead GPS: N47 44.797' / W90 31.498'

The Hike

There is a bonus waterfall just upstream from the state park boundary. It's possible to hike to it from the main waterfalls down by the highway, or start from the bridge on CR 45 (described here). The path leads under the bridge and parallels the river in a distractingly scenic forest of colossal cedar and pine, and ubiquitous aspen and birch, too. Announced with a rumble akin to a bowling ball hurtling toward the pins, the waterfall is just ahead, at the end of a spur trail to the river.

It's fun discovering these seldom-visited waterfalls tucked away up here in the woods, and this one is spectacular, featuring a long, frothy cascade culminating in the whitewater dance at your feet. Watch how the river crashes into the big boulder island in the middle, curving around in a circle and meeting again below. The river slides toward the eastern bank, and a final right turn sends the lively falls to another little drop a short way downstream. From here the river settles down and continues on to its sister falls in the park. The high, rocky cliffs in this gorge add to the already heavenly setting, with many lounge chair boulders close by.

Getting up close with Hidden Falls. BRAYDEN MILLS ▶

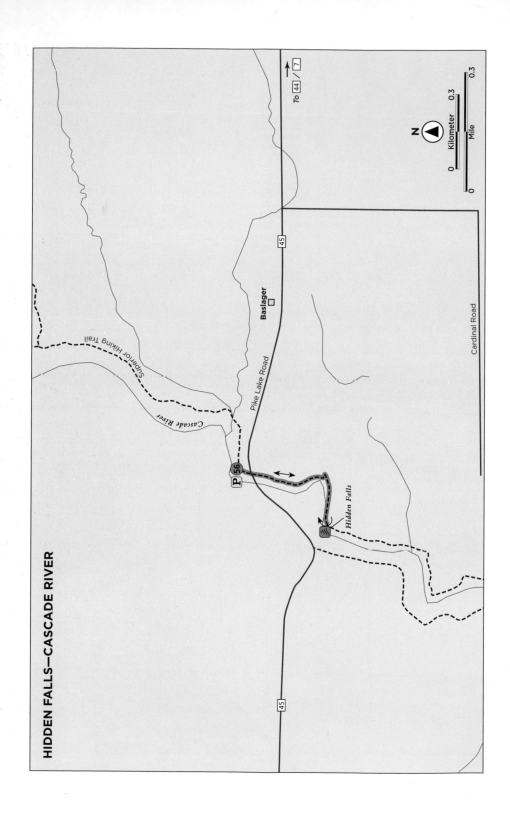

HIDDEN FALLS—CASCADE RIVER

A Cascade River gem secreted away in the woods. BRAYDEN MILLS

The river shows its foamy stuff. JIM HOFFMAN

Miles and Directions

0.0   From the trailhead, follow the path under the bridge, southbound along the river.

0.4   Take the spur trail to the river and waterfalls. Admire the goods and return the same way to the trailhead.

0.8   Arrive back at the trailhead.

57 Rosebush Falls

Named for the wild rose bushes found along this understated Northland river, Rosebush Falls is a hidden treat for North Shore travelers.

Waterway: Fall River
Waterfall beauty: 3.5
Distance: 0.2 mile out and back
Difficulty: Easy
Hiking time: About 10 minutes
Trail surface: Natural
Other trail users: None
Canine compatibility: Leashed pets allowed

Land status: Superior National Forest
Fees and permits: No fee required
Maps: National forest maps;
USGS Good Harbor Bay
Trail contacts: Cook County Visitors Bureau,
116 W. Hwy. 61, Grand Marais 55604,
(218) 387-2524, www.visitcookcounty.com

Finding the trailhead: The Fall River bridge is located 2 miles south of Grand Marais on MN 61, near mile marker 107. Park on the highway shoulder. A skinny trail at the north side of the bridge leads through the woods to the falls.
Trailhead GPS: N47 44.513' / W90 23.250'

The Hike

Lake Superior's North Shore is full of treasures nestled in the crags of cliffs or at the backs of hidden bays. The lake impresses its magic on a grand scale with sunrises filling the horizon, gentle swells that breathe with your soul, or angry storms blasting violently at the shore. Sometimes, though, the vast wilderness booty often appears in smaller, piggy bank–style offerings instead of the entire vault. Rosebush Falls is one of the quiet rewards of a short, unmapped expedition of Superior's riches.

From the north side of the highway, follow the skinny path into a gorgeous stand of white birch, balsam fir, and scattered maple. The trail angles purposefully toward the river and a nice overlook of the waterfall.

Fall River's journey is a short one, with its maiden flows seeping from wetlands up and over the bluffs above Grand Marais. As the river nears Lake Superior, it narrows through a copse of birch and pine and assorted shrubbery to drop 30 feet over a basin of grizzled rock, just 100 feet upstream from the lake. Ancient glacial uplifts pushed the basin's sharp angles and deep fissures up to make a gorgeous view to the northeast. The waterfall holds tight to the rock in a drape of moving water, blurring a background of green algae and moss. A collection of smooth pebbles and football-size rocks flank a small pool below the falls, and in a stone's throw the river meets the lake. Huge and aged cedars adorn the edges of this shallow gorge, fueling the air with their heady aroma.

Rosebush Falls and its craggy gorge. BRAYDEN MILLS

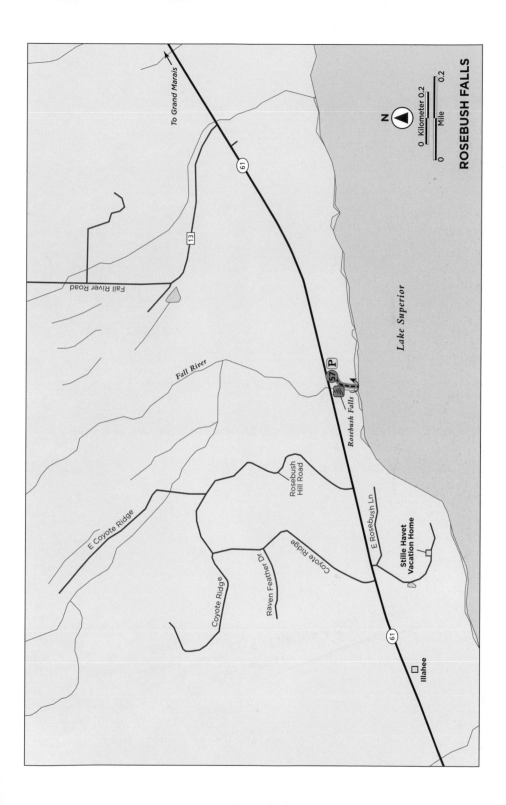

ROSEBUSH FALLS

A Rosebush Falls rainbow. JIM HOFFMAN

Despite this waterfall's proximity to the highway, the setting is secluded and serene. This is one of the best places on "The Shore" to perch on a rock and enjoy the falls, or walk along the boulders and sandbar by the lake. There are superb views of Lake Superior and its scenic shoreline bluffs in both directions. And just 2 short miles down the road is Grand Marais, a treasure trove of its own and a sure bet to capture your attention.

Miles and Directions

0.0 Head off from the highway on the trail into the woods.

0.1 Overlook near the crest of the waterfall. Keep exploring downstream. Depending on water level, it's possible to get close to or even right in the river for a great vantage of the falls. It's also fun to wander to the mouth of the river and Lake Superior.

0.2 Arrive back at the trailhead.

◀ *A foliage-level view of Rosebush Falls.* JIM HOFFMAN

58 Falls of Kadunce River

Carve your very own slice of North Country paradise on this short hike to secluded waterfalls tucked way down in a deep, narrow gorge.

Waterway: Kadunce River
Waterfall beauty: 4.5
Distance: 1.7 miles out and back
Difficulty: Moderate
Hiking time: About 1 hour
Trail surface: Natural
Other trail users: None
Canine compatibility: Leashed pets allowed

Land status: Superior National Forest
Fees and permits: No fee required
Maps: National forest maps;
USGS Kadunce River
Trail contacts: Cook County Visitors Bureau,
116 W. Hwy. 61, Grand Marais 55604,
(218) 387-2524, www.visitcookcounty.com

Finding the trailhead: From Grand Marais, head northeast on MN 61 for 9 miles to the Kadunce River State Wayside. Cross the highway to the Superior Hiking Trail spur trail, which leads to the falls.
Trailhead GPS: N47 47.638' / W90 09.258'

The Hike

The Kadunce River is another North Shore stream often overlooked by the casual observer. The river is hidden away in dense woods and hardly noticed by folks hurrying along the highway. The river's headwaters are part of a cluster of lakes set among high hills about 8 miles inland, and from there the Kadunce flows in a direct route to Lake Superior, largely free of too many sharp bends or time-consuming oxbows. Along the way are several pretty waterfalls, including an ethereal hollow in a deep river gorge.

The trail from the wayside chases the river upstream, gaining elevation to show off a great bird's-eye look at the river and its deepening gorge of pine and birch forest. A short and steep flight of stairs takes you even higher, and the overlook up top offers fantabulous views way down to the constricted depths of the gorge. Descending the steep trail from the ridge leads to river level and a fascinating mini grotto of rock and determined, verdant foliage. The river makes a tight 180-degree right turn here, bending around the nose of the canyon wall.

Back at the main trail and onward to a T intersection, go left for a short foray to another pretty waterfall. This is a tidy little 4-foot plunge just downstream from a wooden footbridge. A sturdy shelf of gray rock secures the waterfall on the trail side, and a higher rock wall shrouded in foliage rises on the other. Pass through this idyllic scene and mosey up to another handsome falls, this one a long tumble over an assortment of rock ledges as the river courses through a deep, narrow gorge. Some

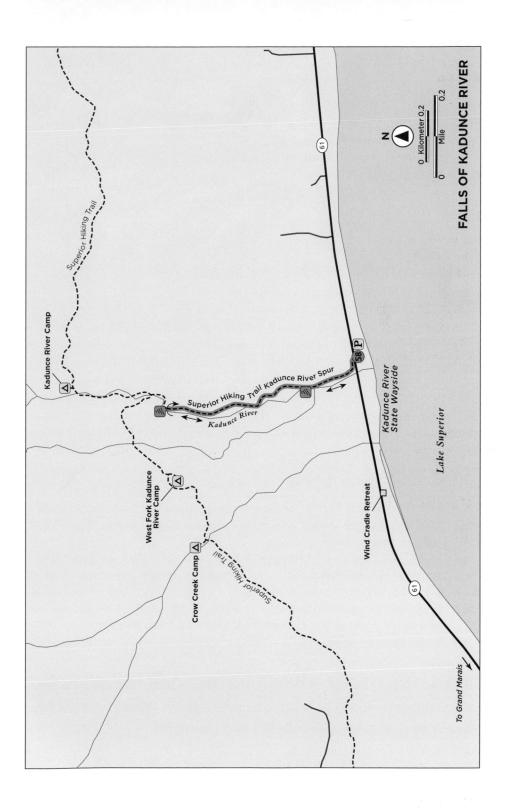

FALLS OF KADUNCE RIVER

The superbly scenic Kadunce River falls. JIM HOFFMAN

of this collection of waterfalls are just a couple feet high, others extend up to 5 feet as they chatter together to make up the main waterfall slide. The view is fine and dandy from right here on the path, but closer access is available with some careful scrambling down to the water. The ledges have created myriad fissures and crests over which the river tumbles in easygoing slides or agitated blasts. The thick woods of birch, maple, pine, and aspen accompanying the river make for a gorgeous setting and another unforgettable, hidden gem of a place to stay awhile and savor the harmony of woods and water.

Miles and Directions

0.0 From the highway and sign for the Superior Hiking Trail spur trail, head into the woods.

0.1 Climb a short section of stairs, following the contour of the ridge as the trail ascends up and away from the river.

0.3 Overlook with a great view of the waterfall. A few dozen steps up the trail, a spur path zigs backward off your left shoulder, dropping steeply to the river. Use caution on this hill. Climb back up to continue on the main trail.

0.8 Junction with the spur trail dropping into the hidden grotto waterfall. A couple more falls are upstream from here; this route returns to the trailhead from this point.

1.7 Arrive back at the trailhead.

Don't miss the sprawling beach at the mouth of the Kadunce River. This is one of the North Shore's best destinations for long walks on the shore, agate and driftwood hunting, or sinking your toes in the sand and stargazing on a warm summer night.

59 Lower Falls–
Judge C.R. Magney State Park

A spur trail splits off on a tangent away from the main path to descend a steep stairway to Lower Falls. Sure, you have to climb back up all those stairs, but this is a great prelude to the bigger falls upstream.

Waterway: Brule River
Waterfall beauty: 4
Distance: 1.4 miles out and back
Difficulty: Moderate
Hiking time: About 45 minutes
Trail surface: Natural
Other trail users: None
Canine compatibility: Leashed pets allowed

Land status: State park
Fees and permits: Fee required
Maps: Judge C.R. Magney State Park map; USGS Marr Island
Trail contacts: Judge C.R. Magney State Park, 4051 E. Hwy. 61, Grand Marais 55604, (218) 387-3039, www.dnr.state.mn.us/state_parks/judge_cr_magney

Finding the trailhead: From Grand Marais, head northeast on MN 61 for 14 miles to the park entrance. The trail starts at the east end of the parking area past the ranger station.
Trailhead GPS: N47 49.189' / W90 03.179'

The Hike

Initially dubbed Bois Brule State Park in 1957, the name changed to Judge C.R. Magney State Park in 1963, in honor of Judge Clarence Magney. In addition to holding title as a lawyer and mayor of Duluth, Mr. Magney was a strong advocate of the state's park system and was very influential in the establishment of state parks and waysides along the North Shore.

From Brule Lake, a giant splotch of blue in the Boundary Waters Canoe Area Wilderness, the Brule River travels through some of northern Minnesota's most beauteous scenery and concludes with three dazzling waterfalls—and a mysterious legend (see Hike 60: Upper Falls and Devils Kettle—Judge C.R. Magney State Park). The path to the falls rises quickly from the trailhead and wanders through gorgeous boreal forest of birch, aspen, spruce, and scattered balsam fir. Forests like this, combined with ample forage like elderberry and alder, provide superb habitat for a thriving wildlife population. Look for white-tailed deer, red foxes, and pine martens at ground level; and in the trees for woodpeckers, jays, chickadees, and many other songbirds. Travel farther to backcountry areas of the park to spot moose, black bears, and even the elusive timber wolf.

After crossing a long bridge over the river, the trail moseys along rolling contours to a spur trail descending steeply to the river and Lower Falls. Ushering the

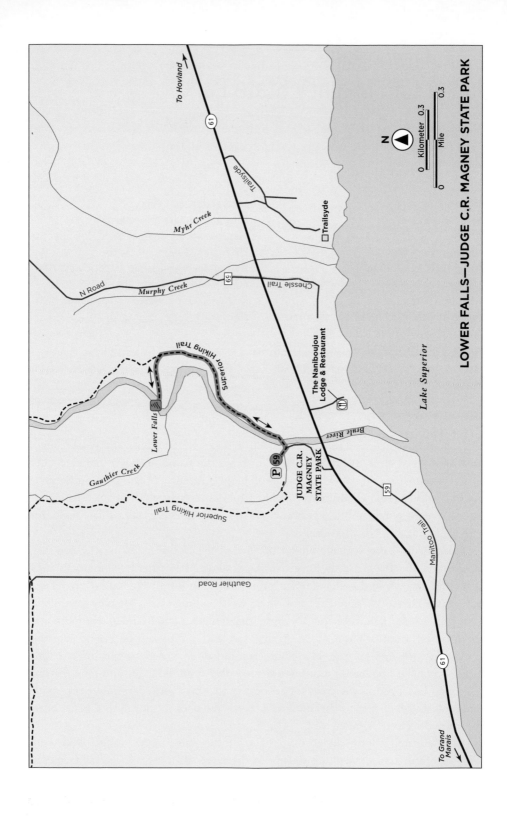

LOWER FALLS—JUDGE C.R. MAGNEY STATE PARK

river sharply around a narrow, rounded bulge of the rocky ridge, this waterfall is a two-step number tumbling 8 feet or so over huge slabs of horizontal rock. Tenacious cedar trees sprout from cracks in the rocks, lending their aromatic ways to the scene.

The river's abrupt bend and the ridge wall hide part of the waterfall from easy viewing, but the sublime setting makes this a rewarding side trip.

Miles and Directions

0.0 Head out on the trail, immersed straight away into vibrant, fragrant, rainbow-hued wilderness. Cross the Brule River on a long bridge.

0.3 Climb a short set of steps with sweet views of the river rapids below.

0.5 Junction with the 0.2-mile spur trail to Lower Falls. Go left and down the steps to the river. Return via the same route.

1.4 Arrive back at the trailhead.

60 Upper Falls and Devils Kettle—
Judge C.R. Magney State Park

Get highlight-reel scenery every step of the way on this exciting hike to the raucous, furious, humbling mystery of Devils Kettle.

Waterway: Brule River
Waterfall beauty: 5
Distance: 2.3 miles out and back
Difficulty: Moderate to difficult
Hiking time: About 75 minutes
Trail surface: Natural
Other trail users: None
Canine compatibility: Leashed pets allowed

Land status: State park
Fees and permits: Fee required
Maps: Judge C.R. Magney State Park map; USGS Marr Island
Trail contacts: Judge C.R. Magney State Park, 4051 E. Hwy. 61, Grand Marais 55604, (218) 387-3039, www.dnr.state.mn.us/ state_parks/judge_cr_magney

Finding the trailhead: From Grand Marais, head northeast on MN 61 for 14 miles to the park entrance. The trail starts at the east end of the parking area past the ranger station.
Trailhead GPS: N47 49.189' / W90 03.179'

The Hike

The path to the falls rises quickly from the trailhead to cross a long bridge over the river. The trail then moseys along rolling contours to a spur trail descending steeply to the river and Lower Falls. Continue on the main trail to an overlook high above Upper Falls. It's a fantastic view, with the falls framed by an accompaniment of dense woods. This is a gorgeous sight throughout the year, but especially in autumn when the entire gorge is ablaze in orange and red. The waterfall drops dramatically in elevation and takes up a good chunk of real estate to do so, beginning its tumble way up around a bend in the river, then splashing down a series of ledges and huge boulders to the final plunge. Farther along the trail is a steep stairway descending straight to the base of the falls. This must be one of the longest sets of stairs on the face of the earth, but the effort is rewarded with an up-close look at the falls. From this point you can see only the final drop, a maelstrom of white foamy water that even in low water seasons provides a misty shower from the spray. A calm pool follows the boisterous activity of the waterfall, and gentle rapids merge back to the more peaceful flow of the river. The trail above, at the top of all those steps, heads over to the excitement of Devils Kettle. Let's go have a look.

As glacial activity in this area eroded more earth than it dumped back in, it formed the rugged gorges and valleys seen today. Ancient basalt and rhyolite lava flows, common to this part of Minnesota, also played a title role in creating this

The Brule River's dramatic Upper Falls. JIM HOFFMAN

High above Devils Kettle. BRAYDEN MILLS

Looking in on the fury of Devils Kettle. BRAYDEN MILLS

stunning landscape. Interestingly enough, beach deposits from glacial meltwater have been found miles inland from Lake Superior's shores, at elevations close to 800 feet above the lake's surface. It's no day at the beach at Devils Kettle, however. The Brule River begins to step lively just upstream, and then rages toward a massive blockade of rock that splits the water into two forks. One plummets into a narrow chute and blasts out to a plunge pool 50 feet below.

The other simply vanishes.

In a raging torrent exploding with frightening velocity, this fork of the river rushes into a gigantic pothole, thundering with the echo of the violent deluge, and is gone. No exit. Local legend insists anything thrust into this void disappears forever, and standing this close to the Kettle one tends to agree. Surely there must be a ghastly labyrinth deep below that burrows through an unfathomable kingdom of rock to Lake Superior. Or is there?

Below the Kettle is a deep, craggy chasm with sheer cliffs rising high above the river. Beyond the tops of the canyon in one direction are open, sunny ridges with distant views of Isle Royale in Lake Superior. Head the other way to swampy lowlands and bogs, or discover lush, hidden canyons in unexpected places. With elevation variations of over 1,000 feet, a remarkable variety of flora and fauna, and a mysterious legend in the mix, this park is a special place and a must-see for your outdoor plans.

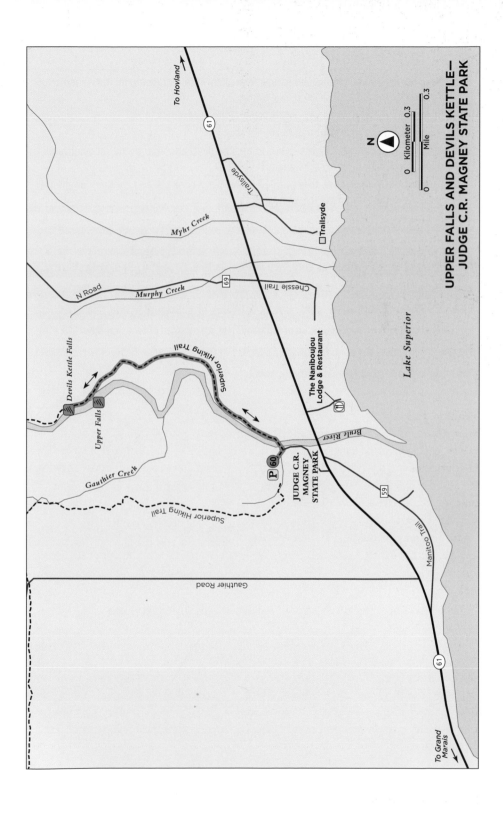

UPPER FALLS AND DEVILS KETTLE—
JUDGE C.R. MAGNEY STATE PARK

Miles and Directions

0.0 Head out on the trail, immersed straight away into vibrant, fragrant, rainbow-hued wilderness. Cross the Brule River on a long bridge.

0.3 Climb a short set of steps with sweet views of the river rapids below.

0.5 Junction with 0.2-mile spur trail to Lower Falls.

0.6 Overlook of Upper Falls, a great place to breathe deep and relax in the moment (and ready yourself for a lot of stairs ahead).

1.1 Descend the long stairway to a river-level view, climb back up, and continue on the trail to Devils Kettle. Return via the same trail.

2.3 Arrive back at the trailhead.

The mystery of Devils Kettle has perplexed visitors to this place since the earliest arrivals. Expert scientists to curious kids have tested and dreamed and theorized and marveled at where on earth all that water goes. Untold bazillions of gallons roar into this giant hole without respite, and no one knows what happens next. All manner of test dummies like Ping-Pong balls, dye, and big ol' logs have been tossed in there, but none have ever resurfaced. Nature is best experienced in mystifying wonder.

61 Portage Falls

Get that off-the-grid vibe with a secluded waterfall and beauteous boreal forest practically within shouting distance of the Canadian border.

Waterway: Portage Brook
Waterfall beauty: 5
Distance: 0.3 mile out and back
Difficulty: Moderate
Hiking time: About 20 minutes
Trail surface: Natural
Other trail users: None
Canine compatibility: Leashed pets allowed

Land status: Superior National Forest
Fees and permits: No fee required
Maps: National forest maps; USGS Tom Lake
Trail contacts: Superior National Forest, Gunflint Ranger District, 2020 W. Hwy. 61, Grand Marais 55604, (218) 387-1750, www.fs.usda.gov/detail/superior/about-forest/offices

Finding the trailhead: From Hovland on MN 61, head north on the Arrowhead Trail (CR 16) for 13 miles to Shoe Lake Road. Turn left and park in the turnout on the left. Hike back across the Arrowhead Trail and take the skinny trail into the woods and to the falls.
Trailhead GPS: N47 59.923' / W90 02.211'

The Hike

A hot tip from a Hovland local led me to this remote waterfall tumbling through the woods just a handful of miles from the Canadian border. The trail descends steeply through dense forest to the river, where the falls cascade over a ledge and drop about 20 feet to another trio of rock tables. This beautiful waterfall is one of the most isolated in the state (my favorite kind). The falls thunder loudly in spring with high water flow and are a truly humbling sight. In fall the river takes on a more demure vibe, and the trees' fiery colors cast the whole scene in a glow.

With the perfect blend of elegantly wild northern forest and an enchanting waterfall, this out-of-the-way gem quickly became one of my favorites.

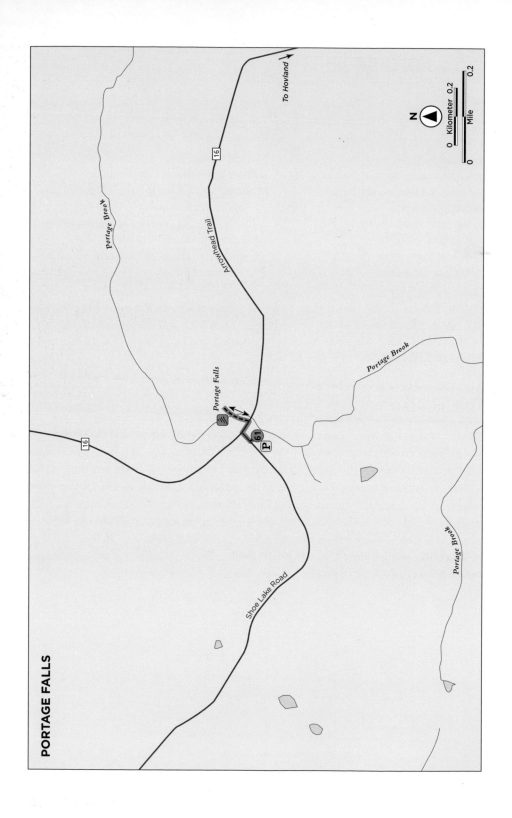

PORTAGE FALLS

Portage Falls is hidden way off the beaten path. BRAYDEN MILLS

Miles and Directions

0.0   From the Arrowhead Trail road, head into the woods on the skinny dirt path. The trail descends rapidly to the stream.

0.1   Arrive at the falls. Retrace your tracks to return.

0.3   Arrive back at the trailhead.

62 High Falls–Grand Portage State Park

American Indians and intrepid voyageurs learned early on to respect the violently beautiful High Falls, tracing the eight-mile Grand Portage with goods and huge canoes. Visitors today can see this stunning waterfall and deep gorge in just a short walk, without carrying a canoe on their backs! High Falls is brilliantly gorgeous in an unforgettable setting. Grand, indeed.

Waterway: Pigeon River
Waterfall beauty: 5+
Distance: 1 mile out and back
Difficulty: Easy
Hiking time: About 40 minutes
Trail surface: Paved
Other trail users: None
Canine compatibility: Leashed pets allowed

Land status: State park
Fees and permits: No fee required
Maps: Grand Portage State Park map; USGS Pigeon Point OE N
Trail contacts: Grand Portage State Park, 9393 E. Hwy. 61, Grand Portage 55605, (218) 475-2360, www.dnr.state.mn.us/ state_parks/grand_portage

Finding the trailhead: Directly south of the Canada-US border on MN 61. From Grand Portage, follow MN 61 north 5.3 miles to the park entrance. The trail to the falls starts at the visitor center.
Trailhead GPS: N48 00.001' / W89 35.525'

The Hike

The Ojibwe Indians named the Grand Portage Git-che O niga-ming, "the great carrying place." This 9-mile overland route served as a link between Lake Superior, the Pigeon River, and beyond to interior lands. The land route was not their first choice, but the river made it clear that there really wasn't a choice. The river flows roughly 30 miles from South Fowl Lake in the Boundary Waters Canoe Area Wilderness to Lake Superior, and the lower 10 miles or so is a succession of torrential rapids, cascades and waterfalls, and huge boulders strewn hither and yon. It is completely unnavigable, especially in a birch-bark canoe, the preference for water travel at the time. Not only that, but the river nears its conclusion in dramatic fashion at High Falls, a 120-foot freefall thundering into a deep gorge. And thus, the "Grand Portage" was made by Indian people for centuries, carrying canoes and supplies on the long path. Early voyageurs utilized the route, as well, transporting goods and fur bundles from Lake Superior inland and back again.

The Pigeon River is the northern boundary of Grand Portage State Park, and the international boundary between the United States and Canada. The park is a unique cooperation between the Grand Portage Band of Chippewa and the State of Minnesota. It is heavily wooded, semi-mountainous terrain of mixed hardwood

Magnificent High Falls and its verdant gorge. BRAYDEN MILLS

and pine, along with white cedar, black ash, and yellow birch. Evidence of the work of spectacular geologic goings-on is visible throughout the park, and one of the most prominent is the park's showpiece, High Falls. The erosion-resistant dike that formed High Falls is a result of massive volumes of basaltic magma that oozed up and leaked all over the place. Many examples of such glacial dikes are evident throughout the park.

An easy, 0.5-mile path leads from the park office to a 700-foot boardwalk, a North Country version of a red carpet. The boardwalk heads gradually uphill to two prominent overlooks of High Falls. And what a sight it is. The river crashes over the edge in raucous thunder, falling onto a ledge below and again down to a deep pool. The massive wall of rock splits a second section of falls that stairsteps in a narrower stream onto a shelf, then plummets to the bottom. Many small rivulets mix in and make their own waterfalls. When the river is running high, it plunges into the black gorge in a 3,200-gallon-per-second deluge. Whatever the mood of the river, this is one spectacular sight—the granddaddy waterfall and the perfect penultimate waterfall of the North Shore's finest.

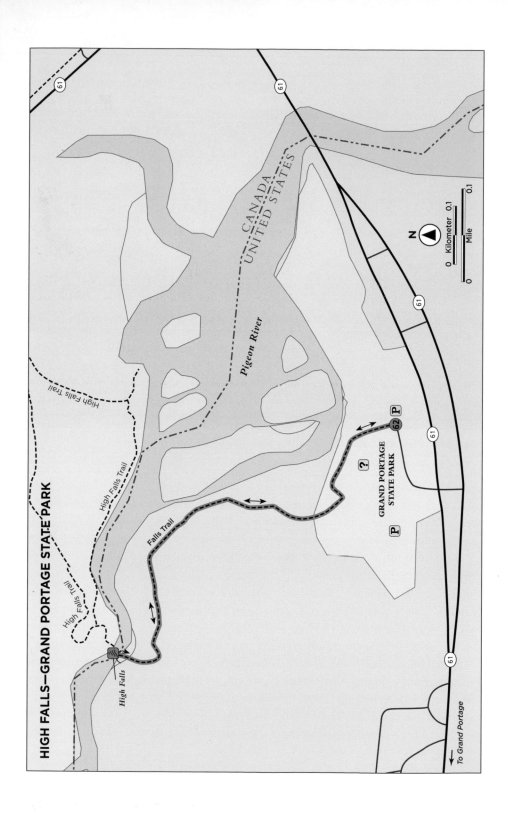

HIGH FALLS—GRAND PORTAGE STATE PARK

High Falls Trail

High Falls Trail

High Falls Trail

High Falls

Falls Trail

Pigeon River

CANADA

UNITED STATES

GRAND PORTAGE
STATE PARK

P

P

62

?

61

61

61

61

61

To Grand Portage

N

0   Kilometer   0.1

0   0.1

0   Mile

Miles and Directions

0.0 From the visitor center, head up the paved and well-marked High Falls Trail. The trail passes through a handsome forest of birch, maple, and spruce fir. A boardwalk takes over as the trail climbs along the ridgeline.

0.5 Arrive at a trio of overlooks with stellar views of the thundering High Falls. Return the same way.

1.0 Arrive back at the trailhead.

Consider a glacier. Imagine, if you will, the unfathomable power of ice. A couple of million years ago, immense glaciers advanced many times from Canada into present-day Minnesota, an icy-cold and immovable legion. The most recent retreating glaciers cut deep gorges and valleys and scooped a really big hole that would eventually become Lake Superior. The rocky ridges you see today around Grand Portage were first visible as just a group of small islands, slowly revealed as the water level receded to create today's big lake.

63 Middle Falls—Grand Portage State Park

Go rugged and deep into the great boreal forest to a pair of frothy and lively waterfalls. Bring a full pack and spend some time with this excitable section of the Pigeon River.

Waterway: Pigeon River
Waterfall beauty: 4
Distance: 5 miles out and back
Difficulty: Difficult
Hiking time: About 3.5 hours
Trail surface: Paved and natural
Other trail users: None
Canine compatibility: Leashed pets allowed

Land status: State park
Fees and permits: No fee required
Maps: Grand Portage State Park map; USGS Pigeon Point OE N
Trail contacts: Grand Portage State Park, 9393 E. Hwy. 61, Grand Portage 55605, (218) 475-2360, www.dnr.state.mn.us/state_parks/grand_portage

Finding the trailhead: The trailhead is on MN 61, directly south of the Canada-US border. From Grand Portage, follow MN 61 north 5.3 miles to the park entrance. The trail to the falls starts at the visitor center.
Trailhead GPS: N48 00.001' / W89 35.525'

The Hike

After High Falls this becomes a strenuous hike, but every step delivers drop-dead gorgeous scenery. An easy, 0.5-mile path leads from the park office to a 700-foot boardwalk, which heads gradually uphill to two prominent overlooks of High Falls. From here the trail clambers over rocks through rugged boreal forest. Some steeper sections with steps roll up and down short hills and ridges along the way, with great views of Lake Superior.

The trail eventually forges through a lowland section to a flat rock balcony overlooking Middle Falls. From a wide, calm stretch, the river plunges about 20 feet into a narrow trough from several directions and explodes at the bottom into a pool. Frothy foam swirls about, and mist from the falls drifts above. A convenient rock peninsula provides easy access and a front-row seat to hang out and watch the show.

A short hike upstream leads to another waterfall, shooting over a 10-foot ledge into whitewater fury. This falls also sports a handy veranda for linger-worthy viewing.

At close to five miles round-trip, this hike demands some extra time, but extra time in Minnesota's far north is a good thing. Fill a backpack with your favorite snacks, bring a good book, and make a day of it.

Misty spray veils Middle Falls. BRAYDEN MILLS

Foam swirls below Middle Falls. BRAYDEN MILLS

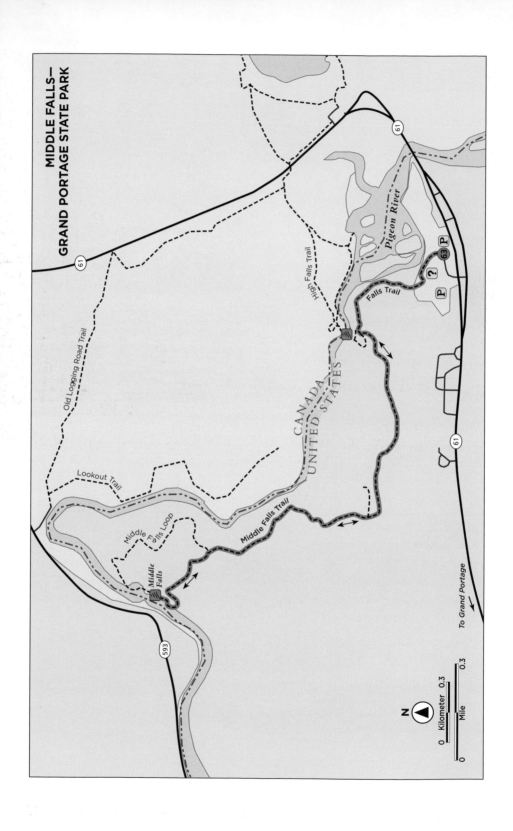

MIDDLE FALLS—
GRAND PORTAGE STATE PARK

Pigeon River

High Falls Trail

Falls Trail

Old Logging Road Trail

CANADA
UNITED STATES

Lookout Trail

Middle Falls Loop

Middle Falls Trail

Middle
Falls

To Grand Portage

61

61

61

593

63

P

P

N

0   Kilometer   0.3

0   Mile   0.3

Quintessential north woods elegance. BRAYDEN MILLS

Miles and Directions

0.0 Follow the High Falls Trail from the visitor center.

0.5 Pass the High Falls overlook trail.

1.3 Great overlook of the river.

2.2 Junction with loop portion of the trail. Go left.

2.5 Arrive at the river and Middle Falls. Continue around the loop or return the same way.

5.0 Arrive back at the trailhead.

Boundary Waters Canoe Area Wilderness and Border Country

The long, serpentine border separating Minnesota from Ontario winds over 300 miles from the Pigeon River in the east to Lake of the Woods in the west. Defining both the actual international border and this spectacular wilderness region are thousands of crystal clear lakes interconnected by miles of streams and rivers and a network of trails and portages utilized by native peoples and pioneers since before recorded history. Once pathways for skilled woodsmen—first the Native Americans, then the valiant voyageurs—many of these waterways became moving highways trafficking millions of board feet of timber used to fuel the building boom associated with westward expansion and industrial growth of the United States in the late 1800s and early 1900s. Thankfully, for those who seek the quiet solitude of a North Country trail or the whisper of a paddle deftly slicing a backcountry waterway, much of this region has returned to its forested splendor, awaiting exploration by foot or water.

The Border Country contains the largest wilderness area east of the Rockies (the Boundary Waters Canoe Area Wilderness [BWCAW] at just over 1 million acres) and Minnesota's only national park (Voyageurs National Park), both of which beg intrepid explorers to ply their watery worlds for hours or days, reaching ever deeper into the wilderness and the primeval world of our ancestors. Chippewa and Superior National Forests, Kabetogama State Forest, and the Minnesota State Canoe Trails on the Big Fork, Little Fork, and Vermillion Rivers provide additional opportunities for adventure. Colorful north woods towns—Ely, Grand Marais, Crane Lake, and others—serve as vacation gateways complete with canoe outfitters, lodges, bait shops, and great places that serve hot grub to modern voyageurs just in from a week or an afternoon in the wilderness.

Here in this land of lakes are nearly countless waterfalls and rapids, many of which live in the lore of history. As many BWCAW waterfalls require access via watercraft, this immense and revered land well deserves an entire book of its own (sequel, anyone?) and is outside the scope of this one. I hope this introduction to Minnesota's wildest watery place whets your appetite to get out there and explore. Here are six favorites accessible with short hikes.

Kawishiwi Falls

Ely is known as the gateway to the Boundary Waters Canoe Area Wilderness. The proud, rugged town has been a wilderness welcome mat for generations and beyond to voyageurs and Native Americans. Just east of Ely, the Kawishiwi River flows into the BWCAW in grand fashion. A short trail through birch and pine forest leads to Kawishiwi Falls, a stunning, frothy beauty rollicking 71 feet over stairsteps of raggedy rock ledges. A couple of viewing areas allow for superb looks at this don't-miss north woods waterfall.

Head east from Ely on US 169 past Winton. At about 4.5 miles, look for the trailhead parking across the road from Deer Ridge Resort.

Dry Falls

There is a second beauteous waterfall a short distance from Ely. A secluded, unnamed stream links Dry Lake and Bass Lake with a double-decker waterfall. Hike the rugged, 2-mile round-trip path from Echo Trail (CR 116) past elevated vistas. Plan for lingering time; there are all sorts of spur trails leading to great views of the waterfalls. Dry Falls drapes over clumps of ancient rock in lacy veils, with a swirling pool between two distinct plunges. A wooden footbridge and fun climbing rocks make this a wonderful destination for extended wilderness time.

Find the falls about 5 miles north of Ely. From US 169, head north on CR 88 to Echo Trail (CR 116). Head north on Echo Trail for 2.4 miles to the Bass Lake Trail parking area and trailhead on the right. Signs point the way to Dry Falls.

Vermillion Falls

Match spectacular north woods scenery with easy access for a full day of waterfalling at the Vermillion River. The series of boisterous falls at the Superior National Forest recreation area on FR 491 west of Crane Lake blasts through bedrock and dense forest. Check it out from handy viewing decks above the river. Don't miss the Vermillion River gorge, a rugged passageway of 50-foot cliffs and aspen-birch-pine forest. Follow a scenic, 3-mile trail from Crane Lake for the best views.

To find the upper falls, follow CR 24 for 1.5 miles south to FR 491. Head west for 5.3 miles to the recreation area entrance. The Vermillion Gorge Trail departs just north of Crane Lake. Travel north past the Crane Lake Ranger Station. Follow the left fork in the road to a parking area on the left. The trail starts at the northwest end of the clearing. Check with the ranger station for trail updates and conditions.

Seagull Falls

Seagull Falls is located near one of Minnesota's most isolated campgrounds, at the terminus of the famed Gunflint Trail, and a launch point to the BWCAW hinterlands. A pair of falls dances among the boulder-strewn Seagull River with easy access from Trail's End Campground, 58 miles northwest of Grand Marais. Nearby resorts and outfitters provide gear and the last hot shower or slice of pizza before extended wilderness trips.

From Grand Marais, follow the Gunflint Trail 58 miles to its terminus. Follow the trail from the campground to the falls.

More Falls Nearby

Big Falls

Big Falls is made up of 0.5-mile stretch of frothy white water dropping more than 40 feet down a series of ledges and slides lined by low rock walls. Gain great views of the whole works from Big Falls Campground on the south side of the Big Fork River.

Find the waterfall at Big Falls Campground; US 71 and Whispering Pines Drive in Big Falls.

Little American Falls

Score guaranteed solitude at this remote and picturesque waterfall tumbling through a steep-walled valley crowned with birch and ash forest. Score the canoe-access campsite on the river's south side for extended stays.

Find the waterfall 8 miles north of Effie on CR 5. Go left at the sign for Little American Falls and follow the road for 0.5 mile to the picnic area.

Hike Index

About the Author

Steve Johnson is a self-propelled recreation junkie and fan of all things outdoors. He grew up roaming the northern lakes and forest regions of Minnesota and Wisconsin and brings four generations of proud family heritage to this exciting book. An avid hiker and cyclist, Steve can usually be found on a hiking trail in the woods somewhere, or with his bike and a wide-open road. With a spare hour or five, he is outdoors and in tune with nature's finest.

A regular contributor to *Backpacker* and other regional magazines across the country, some of Steve's other work includes *Best Bike Rides Minneapolis-St. Paul*, *Loop Hikes Colorado*, *Bicycling Wisconsin*, *Mountain Biking Minnesota*, and spinoff sporting events projects. Don't miss his new children's book, *Jack & Lauren in The Big Bog*. This is his second comprehensive guide to Minnesota waterfalls. Steve lives and writes in southeastern Minnesota and far north Wisconsin.

About the Photographers

Twin Cities–based photographer **Brayden Mills** enjoys hiking and other outdoor pursuits, shooting the best of Minnesota's natural world, as well as downtown music events and video productions. See his work on Facebook at Brayden Mills Photo and Video and on Instagram at @_braydenmills.

Jim Hoffman is an award-winning photographer based in St. Paul. His work has been featured in Minnesota State Park and Bluff Country Region tourism publications and calendars, as well as in *Minnesota in Seasons: A Photographic Journey Through Minnesota*.